Gang Free

Gang Free

Friendship Choices for Today's Youth

Valerie Wiener

Fairview Press   *Minneapolis*

Published by Fairview Press, 2450 Riverside Avenue South, Minneapolis,
MN 55454.

Library of Congress Cataloging-in-Publication Data

Wiener, Valerie
    Gang Free : friendship choices for today's youth / Valerie Wiener
        p.   cm.
    Includes bibliographical references and index.
    Summary: Explores teenagers' constant search for friendship and for
ways to belong to a group and discusses parental involvement in this ever-
evolving process.
    ISBN 0-925190-76-4 (acid free) : $19.95
    1. Friendship in adolescence—United States—Juvenile literature. 2.
Interpersonal relations in adolescence—United States—Juvenile literature. 3.
Parent and teenager—United States—Juvenile literature. [1. Friendship. 2.
Interpersonal relations. 3. Parent and teenager.] I. Title.
BF724.3.F64W54   1995
158'.25'0835—dc20   95-23633
                                                                   CIP
                                                                    AC
First Printing: October 1995

Printed in the United States of America
99 98 97 96 95   7 6 5 4 3 2 1

Cover design: Circus Design

Publisher's Note: Fairview Press publishes books and other materials related to
the subjects of physical health, mental health, and family and social issues. Its
publications, including *Gang Free,* do not necessarily reflect the philosophy of
Fairview Hospital and Healthcare Services or their treatment programs.

For a free current catalog of Fairview Press titles, please call this toll-free
number: 1-800-544-8207.

The value of a book reflects the people who have lived its messages. That's why I am dedicating this book to the hundreds of teenagers who candidly contributed to its content. And . . . to the parents who shared their insights.

Contents

Foreword
by Hugh O'Brian

Youth. To many this appears to be a frivolous time: no cares, no concerns, no responsibilities. Yet it also serves as a time of enormous need for teenagers. It is a period of growth when teenagers search with urgency and commitment for friends—those people who can understand and share their concerns, their confusions, and their confidences.

Not until *Gang Free: Friendship Choices for Today's Youth* was published have we had a resource that could help teenagers and their parents understand how teens develop and seek out friendship. Valerie Wiener has combined the skills of an accomplished journalist, a polished writer, and a youth advocate to explain the teenage friendship process, from societal pressures to the search for security among peers to the need for independence from parents. She has integrated the voices of teenagers and their parents to personalize, from both perspectives, the teenage friendship experience.

Valerie wrote this book with passion to create a dual awareness. Teenagers experience complex adjustments to their changing selves and to others as they seek out friends and join groups. At the same time, parents must accept the associated challenges—and bear the distinctive parental responsibilities—that accompany their adolescents' adjustment to the dynamics of friendship in their quest for adulthood.

For nearly four decades, I have worked directly with teenagers from all over the world. I founded the Hugh O'Brian Youth Foundation because I recognized a distinct need: to bring the world's teen-leaders together in an environment of opportunity and inspiration. Valerie has accomplished something similar with teenagers and parents from diverse backgrounds and ideologies. Her ability to tap into their minds and hearts, to listen to them, to empower them to share their ideas . . . is an inspiration to us all.

Valerie's information and insights, along with the candid comments expressed by teens and parents throughout this book, will prompt all of us to consider teenagers and their evolving friendship needs in new, exciting, invaluable ways. Thanks, Valerie, for having the wisdom to write a book no one else has had the vision to tackle.

—Hugh O'Brian, Founder
Hugh O'Brian Youth Foundation

Preface
It Begins with One

*One plus one. Knowing that there is more to the world
includes more than just you alone.
One plus one. Reaching out to someone else, seeking the
company and support of another person.
One plus one. The beginning of a group.*

Several years ago, one of my teenage nieces asked me if I could share a private moment with her. "Of course," I responded. These intimate dialogues had become very important to me, especially when I recognized how quickly these four girls would zoom through their teens and on into adulthood. But it was not the vision of the future that she needed to discuss. It was the present—a need she had right then.

"Aunt Valerie," the fourteen-year-old nearly whispered, as she searched my eyes for an answer. "Do you know what the most important thing in the world is to me?" I pondered all of the possibilities. Discovering a cure for AIDS? Writing a blockbuster novel? Running the Boston Marathon in record time? Getting into the college of her choice? With all of these possibilities racing through my mind, a mere "no" was the only answer I could voice.

"To be liked" was her immediate response. "I want to be part of the group, and have people like me," she added. "And it's so hard, because I want it to work."

I did not say anything. Listening counts for a lot at times like this. Silence.

It was at that moment when I realized the significant part that friendship and the group process play in the lives of our country's teenagers. Although my niece's personal dilemma tells the story of only one adolescent, it reverberates the inner cry of millions and millions of teenagers.

Both curiosity and a journalist's instinct prompted me to pursue this theme. What I discovered, much to my dismay and disappointment, was the lack of material on the subject of teenage friendships and groups. Somehow, authors who address the issue of friendship have written about preschool playmates, preadolescent buddies, and adult friendships. What happened to the teen years? I wondered. Are these books locked in vaults somewhere, or resting within the realm of an unknown author's imagination? It did not take long for me to realize that parents and teenagers, long held hostage by ignorance about the subject, could benefit from information about friendship and groups. I decided that I would provide the needed material about how teenagers select their groups, and the impact these friends have on their sense of identity and support.

To lay the foundation for my task, I read forty-six books and hundreds of articles. I also conducted original research with 216 teenagers from twenty-two countries, who represented their nations at the Hugh O'Brian Youth (HOBY) Foundation 1993 World Leadership Congress. This survey focused on teen identity and friendship. Of interest, the results throughout the survey tallied almost identically—within two percentage points—for students from the United States and those participants from the rest of the world. So, my references to this study throughout the book will reflect the combined "international" percentages.

To personalize the information even more, I created opportunities to interact one-to-one with teenagers who have established a substantial part of their identities through group membership. I talked with teenagers who primarily identified themselves as members of school clubs like French club, Key club, or choir; religious youth organizations; Students Against Drunk Driving (SADD); athletic teams and lettermen clubs; scouting; minority cultural organizations; antisocial gangs; rural organizations like 4-H; community and school leadership organizations; and accelerated scholastic programs.

Several have no formal group identities at all, although they regularly "hang out with their friends" in social settings. Others identified with people at their places of employment.

I listened to the teens, then I listened to their parents. Contributors talked with me, and expressed their thoughts privately on paper. You will be able to learn about them, too; I have included excerpts of their dialogues throughout the book to illustrate the friendship and the group process.

The teens involved in the one-to-one research will be identified by first name, age, and primary group. HOBY teens, however, participated in the research anonymously, so I only give their gender, ages, and—sometimes—their countries. I identify each contributing parent by first name, as well as the teen's name, age, and primary group. All parents had at least two children; one had eight. So, to ease the understanding of their quotes, I specify only the teenager specifically addressed by the parents' responses.

I have built this book around the intertwining needs of teenagers and parents. That is why I divided it into two parts: Part 1: *How America's Teenagers Make Friends* and Part 2: *Getting Parents Involved.*

With purpose, I have crafted this book to provide both parents and their teenagers with usable information, derived from discovery. Put to use, these ideas can help foster vast opportunities for bridge-building between parents and children. Knowledge provides opportunities to help us in this way.

This book wastes no time in sharing insight. It starts to unfold in chapter 1, where the reader can begin the process of transforming sometimes cross-generational rivals—parents and teenagers—into team champions.

So, let's begin.

Acknowledgments

In 1993, I met with seven teenagers to discuss a book idea I wanted to develop. Their input and energy during our several meetings inspired me to move forward with a book about friendship, identity, and empowerment. So, my first thanks go to Mallie Al-Khafaji, Sloane Arnold, Jeffrey Breeden, Josefine Durazo, Neil Gupta, Terreah Hesler, and Melody Shaw for their insights about emerging adults.

I was also fortunate to receive invaluable assistance from the Hugh O'Brian Youth (HOBY) Foundation. This international organization allowed me to conduct my survey about identity and friendship with its World Leadership Congress attendees. HOBY offered wonderful support, and the 216 participants from twenty-two countries contributed candid responses that reenforce main points in this book.

Several dozen teenagers, who represented diverse youth groups, offered their thoughts to enhance the messages I deliver in this book. I quote forty of them throughout the chapters. Parents of thirty-six teens openly expressed their ideas about involvement with their teens and the groups they join. My thanks to them all.

My ultimate appreciation goes to my proofreaders for the hours they spent poring over this text. Their comments and suggestions reflect their expertise and experiences, as well as strengthen the material. A proud and humble thanks to: Marge Appuglise, Ted Garcia, Sari Greenberg, Neil Gupta, Charlene Herst, Robert Kelch, Ann Lynch, Judy Reich, Dr. George Ann Rice, and Jasmine Wiener.

As with anything, behind-the-scenes people often kept the project moving forward when I wondered whether I would meet deadlines—mine and my publisher's. Victor Carillo served as my partner from start to finish. By title he was my administrative assistant; in reality, he stabilized me when I wondered whether I could pull it all together and deliver the book I wanted to write. When all else failed, he reminded me about the value of humor. To my agent, Ruth Wreschner, a nod of appreciation for believing in me and giving me direction when I needed it most.

My support system also included close friends who maintained their faith in me and encouraged me to write a book that could make a positive difference for parents and their teens. A special thanks to David Katzman and Idora Silver for reminding me often about my mission.

Part 1
How America's Teenagers Make Friends

1
Today's Teenagers
On the Jet Track

Heather peeked over the top of her wire-rims, as she focused her tired eyes on the clock. She clutched the pencil in her hand, creating a noticeable dent in the fingers that embraced it. She bent her head, returning her attention to the seven-page test that sat as a determinable foe on her desk. Battle. Yes, that's an appropriate word to describe the confrontation between the teen and the exam that now challenged her. Although only moments had passed since she read the first question, to Heather it had seemed like hours. Yet, she did not have enough time to answer the remaining pages, not the way she wanted to. She had owned this feeling often. Too much to do. Never enough time. No one, absolutely no one, could feel this way . . . but her.

The Jet-Track Generation

Welcome to the world of teenage jet tracking. That period when adults, especially parents, expect teenagers to super-perform in all of their classes at school, prevail in all of their extracurricular activities, whiz through their chores at home, and socially eclipse every other person in their group. Simply put, today's teenagers are expected to be the superstars of the jet-track generation.

Theoretically, these expectations are possible. They are committed to the pages of an unknown book, written about an ideal world. But in the real world, we have forgotten something very important about our teenagers: They are teenagers, living in a crowded stage of life between childhood and adulthood. These are the years, numbering seven, when no-longer-children-not-yet-adults struggle to find out who they are. During this time, teenagers strive to learn what they should expect of themselves and others who are close and not-so-close to them. They are trying to figure out the whats, whys, and hows in their lives.

> "She is growing up more quickly than she would have on her own, yes. But considering the world she's in, it would be cruel and dangerous to slow her maturation down and leave her a naive victim."
>
> *Barbara, Mother*
> *Mary, 16, SADD*

Teenagers endeavor to understand whether their ideas and actions will ever be noticed, respected or, hope upon hope, make a difference. Each day, every day, our teens struggle to learn as much as they can so that they can take the next step into the adult world. They also face the additional pressures from the outside that compound the growing-up process. This layering of pressure upon pressure is what the jet track is all about.

It would be easy to fall back on the reasons why this jet track has been forged. Some sociologists will put responsibility on dysfunctional or overloaded families. Others will point to the media—with their ability to extend our senses and, ultimately, our experiences beyond the here and the now. Many will trumpet the computer age and a high-stress world, with its nanosecond clock that sweeps us away unknowingly. If given multiple-choice alternatives, "all of the above" would be the right answer.

We need to realize, however, that these multiple sources of fast-paced living—and ultimate expectations of our children—have resulted in our accepting as "normal" the rushing process of our children. We are pushing them out of childhood into adulthood, without a momentary stop in teenhood.

"The world is changing at an incredible pace. Kids are being forced to grow up fast. I would not want to slow down my child's rush into adulthood. Instead, I want to do all I can to help her prepare for success in the very demanding world."

Steven, Father
Ari, 19, Social

We squeeze them through demands for academic excellence. We schedule their nonschool time with accelerated summer camps that concentrate on computer skills, theater, physical fitness, sports, and more adult activities. We book their days, weeks, months, and years so that every passing day is filled with "advancement markers." Yet, have we forgotten that part of this growth process should contain *un*filled time, those periods when teenagers just want—and need—to have fun? In adulthood, this is called *balance*.

At the other end of the spectrum, too many teenagers experience the involvement void—growing up with little or no parental involvement or concern. These adolescents do not have markers, because their parents invest little time or energy in their children's growing up. They set few, if any, standards for their children, and have minimal expectations of, and commitments to, their adolescents.

When society in general, and parents in particular, do expect children to dress, act, and think as adults, we cheat them. We are foisting on them the trappings of adulthood, but not giving them the time they need to adjust to the adult roles we expect them to play.

Some parents ignore the teen years by stereotyping their children. This helps them avoid becoming intimate with their adolescents as individuals. Others sweep children past adolescence, because it is easier to deal with adults than to deal with teens. Still others hurry their teens along because they seek their companionship as equals and as confidants.

"I feel she talks openly with me. She is always willing to

communicate and work out problems. She lifts me up and helps make life easier for me."

Cindy, Mother
Amie, 16, French Club

Whatever the reason, we hurry teenagers into adulthood, yet still impose the limits of childhood. We package them as grown-ups, yet tell them they need to be home by midnight. I am not saying that parents should avoid setting limits, which, of course, they must. Rather, we are creating and transmitting confusing messages to our teens. When adults confuse, ignore, fail to support, or stymie teenagers, these adolescents turn elsewhere for support. Their friends, who would play an important part in their development anyway, take on an even more important role. Just like them, their friends are also zooming through life on the jet track.

Beyond the Home . . . Friends

The relationship between parent and teen reaches a peak of one-sidedness during this era of the child's personal development. Parents expect responsible behavior from their children and, in turn, grant privileges. However, teenagers are not positioned to seek or demand that their parents think or act responsibly, and adolescents do not have the power to punish or reward their parents. Teens can turn to other teens to establish equal relationships. When selecting their friends, teenagers can begin to expect certain thought patterns, behaviors, and degrees of loyalty from their peers.

With their friends, teenagers experience their first, real reciprocal relationships, both as givers and receivers of the fruits of friendship. For many adolescents, this marks the first time they experience mutuality in a relationship.

"I want a friend who can be straight with me. Someone who can be trusted and someone who will trust me."

Chris, 17, Wrestler

"Friends should be fun, understanding, be there when I need them, and need me to be a friend to them."

Jenny, 16, Scholastic

"I expect honesty, dedication, and trust—both ways. I want someone who will stand by me, no matter what is going on or what we're going through. Also, I want someone who will let me into her life, without my having to force myself in. In the same way, she must be trustworthy so that I can share my heart with her."

Mallie, 18, Leadership

Commitment and loyalty also emerge in these early friendships. Teens demonstrate *commitment* by the virtual determination between the friends to keep the friendship alive and working. *Loyalty* enhances this process when either of the friends, or the group itself, is challenged from the outside. However, the results of the 1993 survey I conducted with the Hugh O'Brian Youth Foundation (HOBY) emphasized one standard for friendship above all. These teenagers—216 of them, from twenty-two countries (including the United States)—overwhelmingly listed *trust* as the most important ingredient of friendship. A true friend, according to survey results, is a person you can trust with your time, your feelings, and your most personal thoughts.

When searching for other words to describe friendship, dictionaries certainly lack the breadth, and often simplicity, to describe what friendship can mean to the teenage givers and receivers in these special relationships. Some of the HOBY teens from outside the United States said they consider a friend as someone who:

"forms part of you and is always there for you."

Boy, 16, Mexico

"has time for you, all of the time."

Girl, 17, Ireland

"can share secrets and personal goals with you."

Boy, 16, Malaysia

"understands our sorrows and difficulties."

Girl, 14, India

"will listen to anything you say and still be your friend."

Boy, 15, Italy

"always listens and makes me comfortable."

Girl, 15, Germany

"means as much to me as my family."

Boy, 16, Argentina

"cares enough to wake you up if you are asleep during a fire alarm."

Girl, 16, Amsterdam

The responses from more than 150 fifteen- and sixteen-year-old high school sophomores, from across the United States, were not so different. They consider a friend someone who:

"connects with you emotionally."

"believes in you, in good times and bad times."

"sticks by you and defends you, even through the toughest and most embarrassing moments."

"lets and encourages you to be yourself, in the highs and the lows, and is someone you can encourage to do the same."

"will make sacrifices for you, including die for you."

"spends quality time with you."

"has a place in your life as a long-time soul mate."

"makes a positive impact on my life."

"sees me and loves me, even though I screw up."

"creates a relationship based on mutual respect and openness."

"knows what you are thinking before you do."

"will catch you when you are falling."

"listens to you, gives you advice, and doesn't tell anyone else."

"encourages you to talk about religion or politics, and will still call you a friend when you are done."

"leaves a footprint on the memory of your life."

The Lessons of Friendship

Friendship can offer a sustaining force in the life of a teenager. It serves as the lifeblood for the ups and downs of daily living. Early friendships have a very potent effect on a teenager's sense of self and personal development. This is especially true for so many teenagers who use relationships outside the home to define themselves.

One good example involves the vast number of teenagers who do not live in the traditional family—with both parents happily married to each other. For millions of teenagers this family does not exist. These teenagers, like many others with different reasons, learn to turn to their friends for human bonding. They rely on these relationships for continuity, security, and understanding.

> "When you only have one parent at home, and she has to work to support the family, friends become a lifeline. I look for people who really care about what I have to say. I need friends who will stand by me whatever decisions I make, and advise me if they disagree with something I do."
>
> *Jasmine, 16, Scholastic*

Early into their friendships, teenagers learn an important lesson: To have good friends is not a birthright. Friendship takes practice. Teenagers will stumble and make mistakes; both actions give direction in the friendship process. Even when choosing to make friends in a "controversial group," teenagers can learn important lessons in friendship-building.

> "I expect him to watch my back and not disrespect me. And I want him there if I need him. Someone who won't rat on me."
>
> *Jeremy, 17, Gang*

Another important realization about friendship-building involves growth. Teenagers physically grow at different rates. They also mature differently. Part of the reality of friendship, then, requires teenagers to learn what they can expect from each other, both physically and emotionally. Simply, they must foster real expectations of their friends, and know that every friend cannot meet every expectation they might have.

This awareness does not mean that teenagers should shun each other when their friends do not meet their expectations. It means that the value of friendship involves the knowing— the realization that—just like them, friends can stumble. So to prevent or, at least, cushion that fall, teenagers need to recognize how much they can expect of themselves and their friends. To help establish appropriate standards for lasting friendships, teenagers can and should expect not only the previously mentioned trust, commitment, and loyalty but also *consideration* and *respect*.

Another interesting lesson about teenage friendships involves the importance of best friends during these turbulent years. Having a best friend might seem appropriate at times, especially when they need to be able to confide totally in another person. However, it does not take long for most teenagers to realize that they often have more than one best friend. In fact, it can be perilous—and unrealistic—to expect one friend to satisfy all of another person's needs. This expectation can result in disappointment as well as bruised feelings. Often, to avoid this, most teenagers cultivate several close friendships, each with their own levels of expectations and development. This is the group.

"Friends in my group recognize each person is important to all of the others. We're serious about making and keeping valuable friends."

Lisa, 16, Leadership

"I look to my friends for honesty. I want friends who won't be judgmental of me or my other friends. Friends stand up for what they believe, and are not afraid to have fun."

Jennifer, 16, Social

Teenagers also learn, through trial and error, that friendships usually go through cycles of closeness and distance. Good friends recognize that friendship can fluctuate as expectations, moods, and other needs change. They might experience friendship as an active participant one day, and as a distant spectator the next. The ups and downs of friendship constitute a process. When teenagers realize this, they have a better chance to recognize that these yo-yo experiences are not unique; they are normal.

Dynamic Friendship

Friends who answer each other's needs in sensitive and creative ways have learned that variety and diversity help keep friendships active and strong. This helps teens appreciate the value in having more than one friend at a time.

Some friendships are *single-purpose* friendships. These include the people with whom teens share a limited range of interests or activities. This might include membership in a photography club, participation in a competitive sporting event, or working together at a part-time job. Others are *multipurpose* friends, the people with whom teens want to share a large part of their lives. Multipurpose friends comprise the types of friendships that teenagers usually form. Adolescents often share school life, beyond-school activities, social time, secrets, and more with their friends.

Whichever type of friendship each person satisfies, friendship itself has its own dynamics. Each friendship will contribute something very special to each teenager. . . . Just as that teenager contributes something very distinctive to each friend. These friendships should complement one another, not compete for time, attention, or loyalty.

Dynamic friendship requires that teenagers nurture their friendship bonds with others by maximizing the positive influences, while at the same time minimizing the negative ones. Interestingly, one of the best ways for teenagers to learn this two-pronged technique involves their observing their parents and other adults. What should they look for? *Total communication.*

Teenagers need to observe friends who listen attentively, respond honestly, and ask for input from the other person. The total communication process requires give and take. It empowers teenagers to explore ideas beyond themselves, as well as learn how to expose their own vulnerabilities to people they want to trust.

> "The return of the love, listening, and understanding that I give them."
>
> *Suzy, 15, Rural*

> "The ability to understand what I say and what I feel, what I really mean when I say something vague, companionship, and the ability to make me laugh."
>
> *LiAn 16, Scholastic*

Total communication also helps teenagers actualize their own human potential. It helps them work from within themselves. It enhances their relationships with others, and answers several basic needs that I will explain in more detail throughout this book. These fundamental psychological requirements, according to Dr. Don Dinkmeyer in his book, *Raising a Responsible Child* (Fireside Book, 1973), are the needs to

be loved and accepted
be secure and relatively free of threat

belong and to identify themselves as part of a group
be approved and recognized
move toward independence, responsibility, and decision-making

According to my research, other basic psychological concerns teenagers confront include the needs to

distinguish their own individuality
share time, space, and interests with others
develop definitions and applications for reward, punishment, success, and failure
recognize their potential to make a difference

Also to progress in the environment of dynamic friendship, teenagers will want to pay attention to the *process* of friendship. This involves physical changes, emotional exchanges, psychological shifts, and more. It requires open, unselfish exchanges between friends that might challenge a teenager's patience. The rewards parallel the effort. Effective give-and-take between friends will help ensure a stronger, more enduring friendship with each interaction.

"I expect friends to be honest, and to be good listeners. I don't want them to tell other people anything that I don't want to be repeated. I want my friends to have respect for me, my other friends, and their parents. I want them to expect the same from me."

Heather, 15, Religious

Another interesting aspect about developing a dynamic friendship requires taking risks. During this seven-year period, teenagers normally want to test their limits. Naturally, this includes testing the limits of their friendships, too. Parents and other adults should encourage adolescents to take advantage of opportunities to challenge themselves and their own thinking. Teenagers should challenge their friends, even when they might disagree with each other; friends are entitled to disagree. In fact, by exploring new ideas, teenagers can inspire in each other new interest areas, thus adding new vitality to their friendships.

Quick Points

- Today's teenagers travel on the jet track. We, as a society, expect them to be super-performers in everything they attempt, from school and home responsibilities to social activities.
- The jet track has resulted from a combination of factors: modern family dynamics, the media, high-tech living, and more.
- Jet-tracking our teenagers means that we accept as "normal" the rushing process that jumps our teenagers from childhood into adulthood, with little or no time to treat the teen years as a distinct process.
- Adults, especially parents, rush teenagers past adolescence into adulthood. Yet, these same adults still impose the limits of childhood on their teenagers.
- Some parents, however, set few—if any—standards for their children. They have minimal expectations of, and commitments to, their children. This results in the *involvement void*, which stifles adolescent development.
- Teenagers value commitment and loyalty in their friends. Most important, however, trust tops the list of friendship priorities among teenagers around the world.
- Friendship serves as a lifeline between teenagers, often serving as a primary source for personal development.
- Even mistakes in selecting friends help teach lessons about friendship.
- Teenagers grow physically and emotionally at different rates, and this will influence the nature of their friendships.
- Teenagers can reap benefits from having several close friends.
- Friendships go through cycles of closeness and distance.

- *Dynamic friendships* require that teenagers nurture their friendship bonds with others. This requires maximizing the positive influences, while, at the same time, minimizing the negative ones.
- Dynamic friendships also thrive on risk-taking.
- Teenagers can learn a lot about friendship by observing others.
- Total communication helps teenagers work with themselves and others to answer several basic psychological needs.
- Friendship is a process that involves physical changes, emotional exchanges, psychological shifts, and more.

2
The Power of Self

Randy reread the article he had finished writing for the high school newspaper. He looked at its headline one more time: "Teenager Abandons Self in Search of Self." In crafting the concise message of that headline, Randy realized that his classmate's search was something that had been tempting him, too, for a very long time. Although the story focused on a classmate, Randy knew that he could have written it as a personal essay. One more time, he ventured into the text:

> One local teenager has discovered a way to ease the confusion of growing up. He has decided to start over. This time, according to Normal Ado Lescent, "I'm going to do it right."
>
> Lescent said, "I will figure out who I am, and what I expect of myself, my parents, and my friends. I will also try to get an idea about what I want to do with my life." The innovative teenager is giving his personal renovation plan thirty days to kick in.
>
> To accomplish his goal, Lescent said he will discontinue all friendships; quit all clubs; start his classes over; avoid television, movies, radio, and video games; and communicate with other people only when necessary. "This should help me clear my head, get a new start, and finally figure out who I am," Lescent said confidently.

Of course, this excerpt is fiction. The need for teenagers to learn about themselves, however, is not. This driving force underscores one of their greatest needs to know. By learning about who they are and what they expect of themselves, and others, teenagers can develop worthwhile friendships that enrich everyone.

One of the greatest resources for teenage learning involves observation—watching how other people act and react. Adolescents learn to model themselves after people they admire. For most teenagers, these early role models are their parents. From infancy, children create their self-images based, in large part, on how their parents handle and care for them. The HOBY survey reinforced this point: Fifty-nine percent of the respondents consider their parents the most important influence in their lives.

Teenagers learn early to watch what their parents say and do, as well as what kinds of results these communication efforts produce. As they grow older, teenagers learn to broaden the expanse of their people watching. They also learn that something else takes place when they watch others. At the same time teenagers are peering outward at others, they are also looking inward at themselves. Consciously or subconsciously, they are weighing whether these same thoughts, attitudes, actions, and reactions will work for them.

It is normal for teenagers to develop in this way. They are not weird or weak; they simply are not yet sure of what to say or do in certain situations. This learning process is much more sophisticated. It includes observation, understanding, evaluation, and response.

As teenagers experience this transformation, they naturally begin to learn about the self, the individual each of them is, from the inside out. So, why do they need to understand the "real self?" What is the value in knowing why they say and do certain things, or act and react in particular ways? Why will it help them to study practical applications of self concepts? The answer is simple: to have positive control over their lives.

Yes, teenagers are probably burned out on words like self-esteem, self-worth, self-value, self-development, and others. What do these words mean, anyway? Can adults really know what teenagers think about themselves and what is happening in their lives? Who cares? I do. After thirty years as a professional communicator, I know that teenagers have an unlimited source of power within themselves. This resource can help them set the direction of their lives and propel them to wherever they want to go, starting right now.

To begin this journey, teenagers need to understand how to read the map for their life's adventure. This will require them to make a strong commitment to self-exploration. They can start by recognizing just how terrific they already are. Realizing and applying this knowledge, even during the tough times, teens will be able to deliver their messages, make their personal connections, and soar.

So Who Am I?

How do teenagers initially define themselves? By how tall they are, the color of their hair, the size of clothing they wear? Teenagers demonstrate great sensitivity about their looks. They care about their appearance and its impact on how people respond to them.

Mira Kirshenbaum, in her book, *Parent-Teen Breakthrough* (Plume, 1991), responds to the universal question of teens, "Who am I?" by listing some of the ways teenagers create reference points for their identities. A sample of this list: style of dress, religion, politics, music preferences, sexual orientation, where the teen lives, the teen's level of ambition, and what the teen likes to do for fun.

Two additional, interrelated criteria that help define teenagers and the identities they seek involve the people they choose as friends, and the groups they join for companionship. These milestone influences underscore the reason I decided to write this book.

As adolescents pursue answers to the "Who am I?" question, one message will be clear. Whatever criteria teenagers might select to create a personal identity, they will achieve a distinctive identity with many components. Parents need to remember that this process is a normal one for adolescents.

The search for self serves an integral purpose in the definition of adolescence.

> "It is very important to be fairly secure about who you are and to have a degree of confidence. I'm in a leadership or intellectual group. The environment is very competitive and backstabbing. So, to survive, it is essential to believe in who and what you are."
>
> *Karim, 17, Leadership*

> "Oddly, I don't have such a positive self-image. I am out-going in selecting friends and the things that I do, but I don't think I value myself enough. I don't really like me, but I never portray that part of me to my friends."
>
> *Xochitl, 20, Cultural*

> "I'm a very determined and outgoing person. There are times when I don't feel very good about myself and my appearance, but that's a natural part of growing up. You need to have a confident view of yourself to make honest friends."
>
> *Amber, 14, Social*

Teenagers frequently start their journey into self-identity by determining who they are *not*. Initially, this often determines that they do not want to be anything like their parents.

So, the search begins. On this journey, most teenagers admit that they get some of their strongest impressions about themselves and interpersonal relationships from the media, especially television and magazines. In particular, commercials help them define themselves. Teenagers are told what kind of shoes will make them cool, what kind of deodorant will enhance their popularity, and what kind of gum will attract dates.

Unfortunately, the real world sketches a different picture for our teens, in spite of their loyal commitment to these popularity elixirs. No doubt, despite all of their efforts, teens will still get their shoes dirty, perspire at the most awkward moments, and experience bad breath after eating onion rings. Teens should remember that advertisers reinforce every message with one mandate: Spend your money. Advertising is a very competitive business, and sometimes advertisers will make undeliverable promises. After all, they do not have to look into the faces of teenagers when disappointment tumbles their world.

The media, through entertainment and commercials, also presume that all teenagers develop at the same rate in the same ways. Not true. Even if adolescents and their best friends were born on the same day, at the same hour, in the same hospital, each would mature in different ways. When teenagers accept this fact, they can reduce the sting of many of the social discomforts they experience.

Once teenagers recognize the impact of modern technology on the visions they have of themselves, what else defines who they are? It is really a composite of their bodies, their minds, and their emotions. They cannot always control any or all of these factors at any one time.

Equally important and exciting, however, teenagers do have total control in one way. They can control how they *respond* to these influences. When they develop positive self-perceptions, adolescents will recognize the fleeting nature of conditions in their lives. They will realize that some influences have the potential to disappear as they themselves mature. For example, teenagers will not always get blemishes, write seemingly meaningless essays, or feud with their brothers and sisters.

Self-Esteem

Teenagers probably think that the whole world knows what is going on in their heads, no matter what they do to protect themselves. The more they try to display confidence in what they do, the more they stumble at the most inappropriate times.

At this time in their lives, teenagers may feel especially vulnerable about their self-confidence. They may see themselves figuratively bouncing like a basketball. They experience all of the ups and downs. At one moment, he is the person who confidently walks into the post-game dance. At the next moment, she is the person who is uncomfortable when boys look at her for two seconds too long. He may have enough confidence to pull an A on a test, and, sixty seconds later, be reluctant to tell a friend how well he did. This is normal.

Part of this discomfort comes from confusion. Teenagers often demonstrate different selves at different times, and with different people. Sometimes teenagers will want to keep parts of themselves, and how they think, private from their best friends. Yet they might be eager to share these same important messages with someone else—even a stranger.

Inner confusion runs rampant in adolescents. Sensitivities reign. Teenagers tend to be secretive because of fear—often, the fear of ridicule. They can also be irritable because they intensely dislike interference from other people who cannot really understand them. Sometimes they act cocky, because they need a cover-up for times when they are uncertain. Down times also strike teenagers with great regularity, because they often interpret life as a conspiracy, when nothing seems to go right. Rebellion and defiance also invade the lives of teenagers. Teens feel the need to challenge the rules, and be left alone to figure things out for themselves.

"We have come to accept that authority and rules are necessary as they guide us to success."

Neil, 17, Employment

"Anything within reason is okay. Anything utterly absurd calls for rebellion!"

Natalie, 17, Choir

"I don't like it when my parents tell me to stay home when *they* never listened to rules."

Jessie, 14, Gang

"This is almost an essential part of my everyday life. Respecting the rules laid down not only by my parents but everyone else is very important to me. Coming from

England, with English grandparents living with me, respecting authority is also very important."

Reza, 16, Scholastic

Learning how to balance outside rules and self-rule helps teenagers take control and responsibility of their lives and develop a healthy self-esteem. What is self-esteem, anyway? Dr. Nathaniel Branden, an early pioneer of the self-esteem movement, describes the concept in his book, *The Power of Self-Esteem* (Health Communications, Inc., 1992). He defines self-esteem thus:

> The experience that we are appropriate to life and to the requirements of life. More specifically, self-esteem is *confidence* in our ability to think and to cope with the basic challenges of life. Self-esteem is confidence in our right to be happy, the feeling of being worthy, deserving, entitled to assert our needs and wants, and to enjoy the fruits of our efforts.

Obviously, self-esteem means more than an inherent sense of self-worth. It includes powerful human need, essential to teenagers and their becoming who they are, as well as influencing who they want to become. *Empowerment.*

When teenagers have real confidence in themselves and in what they think and do, they are empowered. By continuing to be aware of this and other qualities in themselves, teenagers can find energy and motivation to face challenges, complete tasks, and respond positively to relationships. They can enjoy satisfaction from what they think, say, and do. They thrive.

"I feel really good about myself. I'm not conceited. I just don't have any hang-ups about life or about myself."

Amy, 15, Religious

"I feel better about myself now that I am in a gang."

Jessie, 14, Gang

"My self-esteem is pretty high. So, if a group is going to bring me down I don't want to be there. When picking a group, you have to look for one that is on the same level you are."

Paul, 19, Cultural

Teenagers need to realize, however, that they are not bestowed with self-esteem. They need to develop it. Self-esteem is not static. Anyone can challenge it at any time, any place. In fact, the more choices and the more decisions a person needs to make—whether to do drugs, break curfew, call home about being late, not drive while drinking—the more crucial will be the need for self-esteem.

As teenagers grow and nurture their self-esteem, their choices will expand. Teens will demonstrate willingness, and probably eagerness, to venture beyond their *safety zone*—their own place of personal comfort—and try new things, in new ways, with new people. As adolescents experiment, they will often fall short of perfection, or even success, as defined by others, especially their group. However, the very fact that teenagers are willing to venture beyond "the known" produces success in itself.

"Being the member of a particular group helps you get to know other people and realize what kinds of people are out there."

Charla, 15, SADD

"Picking a group is very important. I know I should be careful not to narrow myself. In order to make it in this country we need to work with people from all groups, colors, and races."

Mayte, 19, Cultural

"I think it is important to share time and interests with others so your group can get to know you well."

Jason, 17, Gang

Let me issue a warning at this point. Self-esteem does not license teenagers to sing their personal praises in the mirror every day. Nor should they brag to anyone else who will listen. They also cannot demonstrate self-esteem merely by joining a popular club or hanging around with the "right people." Although teenagers have a right to be proud of high self-esteem, they should not flaunt it.

Neither can a teenager's heritage, racial background, or family achievements define self-esteem. Teens cannot rely on these cosmetic considerations to define who they are. To work for them, self-esteem must come from *within each person.*

> "I am strong, good, and quick-witted. I am okay with who I am as an individual. This is important for self-identity."
>
> *Mary, 16, SADD*

Teenagers need to put self-esteem to work honestly and responsibly, especially when it involves the feelings of others. Self-esteem is a very personal experience about what people think of themselves. Teenagers cannot define it by what and how others think about them. So they need to be careful not to fall prey to becoming "approval-seekers." Adolescents should not let how others behave toward them solely define how they think about themselves. Sixty-three percent of the participants in the HOBY survey indicated that they generally turn to themselves first for respect. Parents—with twenty-three percent—were the next most important source for teens in their search for respect. Only six percent of the HOBY teens considered peers their most important source of respect.

Other people's feelings about a teenager can be unpredictable, with the potential to produce great heartbreak and disappointment for that tender teen. When Terri brought home her report card of A's and B's, with one C, her parents did not congratulate her on pulling good grades in advanced courses. Instead, they questioned why she got a C in art.

Terri, an approval-seeker, found herself dwelling on her parents' negative response about one class, rather than commending herself for performing well in six other classes. This response left her emotionally bruised for days.

When teenagers have a healthy sense of self-esteem, they can demonstrate this to other people in many ways. Body language—posture, mannerisms, gestures, expressions—project that teens have a strong dose of self-appreciation. Forthrightness and honesty will position teenagers positively with themselves and others. How adolescents give and receive compliments, as well as criticism, reflects self-esteem. A teen's willingness to be curious, open-minded, and adventurous enhances self-esteem. A good sense of humor, assertiveness, flexibility, and good judgment are also powerful self-esteem tools. These, plus honest self-awareness and well-earned self-pride, help teenagers realize that they do not need to make themselves appear superior to others to elevate themselves.

> "I have accomplished a lot and have high self-esteem. I think my friends should feel the same way about themselves so we can share in our successes and cultures."
>
> *Neil, 17, Leadership*

Self-acceptance also contributes to self-esteem. This does not mean that teenagers have to remain ever-constant and stay the way they are right now. It means that they are empowered to experiment. They can make changes in their lives, and have confidence in themselves for having said or done something new. For example, a teenager might express an original idea in English class, without worrying about what other classmates might think. Or a teen can go to a history museum without wondering how friends might react, or . . . write a letter to the school newspaper, without questioning the right of self-expression.

With enhanced empowerment, teenagers can become responsible for all aspects of their lives. These include their goals, their actions, their ideals, their decisions, their personal happiness, and their relationships. Esteem and empowerment do not come easily, and often the struggle to develop them can be an overwhelming task for a teenager. Defeat—or the perception of defeat—can discourage teenagers from attempting empowerment. However, the concept of "one plus one" I mentioned in the preface applies to esteem and empowerment: One success plus one success is the beginning.

In the real world, self-esteem helps teenagers trust themselves and their own decisions. They can face challenges realistically. They also recognize that they can and do make a difference with their thoughts, actions, and reactions. Self-esteem will encourage lifelong learning, as well as teaching. Teens with high self-esteem can express their autonomy, while appreciating the value of other people in their lives.

> "I feel that I am in a comfortable position with myself and others. I am usually content and secure with myself."
>
> *Jonathan, 17, Religious*

> "I am fairly happy with who I am. I think high self-esteem does affect a person's outlook on friendship. When you care about yourself, you tend to care about the type of friends you choose."
>
> *Alyssa, 15, Letterman*

Independence, Autonomy, and All That Stuff

During adolescence, teenagers experience mixed feelings about their independence. Sometimes, they want their parents, teachers, and other adults in their lives to make decisions and be responsible for them. At other times, teens resent their own dependency on their parents. This occurs especially when parents encourage their children's dependence on them—including everything from giving their teens rides to school to granting them permission to go to parties.

It is normal for adolescents to crave independence. It is normal for them to want enough space to make their own decisions. It is normal for them to want choices in matters that affect their lives. It is normal for them to want to use sources outside the home. It is normal for them to resent being bombarded with too many questions. It is normal for them to be confused about, and struggle with, the role of their parents—the primary authorities in their lives.

In fact, teenagers are positioned in the middle of a revolution—their own mini-war. They are struggling with who they were as children, the people others expect them to be as teenagers, and that person each of them wants to become as an adult. Teenagers are immersed in pushing and pulling—a tug-of-war—that can leave them feeling frustrated and angry. Fortunately, they are not alone. Their friends are also experiencing this personal earthquake.

I learned this message when I spearheaded one of my high school reunions. About a dozen of my classmates and I met to plan the three-day event. After a lot of catching up with each other's lives, we began to talk about how we felt about our high school years. One classmate, who had worn crowns at more than one prom, said she felt totally insecure and unpopular throughout high school. She dated one of the most popular guys in high school, yet, felt that he had only dated her because he felt sorry for her.

Another classmate told us that he felt like a failure on the basketball court, and could not run plays the way they should be run. Yet he was captain of the team and the top scorer. Still another person said that he never felt smart enough to talk with people; he graduated in the top one percent of the class.

Most adolescents will spend their teen years searching for their most prized possession: personal identities. During the teen years, parents assert great interest to prepare their adolescents for the future. However, simultaneously, teenagers will do everything they can to assert themselves to do things their way. Often, many of the steps teens take will be going in a particular direction for the first time. With this travel on new paths, teens will also find ways to improve their self-esteem when it is challenged.

Upgrading Self-Esteem

Even when teenagers have generally high self-esteem, they will have experiences that prompt not-too-good feelings about themselves. This can happen when they are sick, tired, overloaded, or living through important changes. Questions might pop up, such as: "What's wrong with me?" or "Why do things like this always happen to me?" or "I'm not strong enough or smart enough to handle this problem."

Teenagers need to appreciate their capabilities. Equally important, they should not shortchange themselves when faced with challenge. In moments of vulnerability, parents must encourage adolescents not to quit on themselves.

To reinstate their self-esteem, teenagers will need to take action. Self-esteem does not just happen. Parents and other adults need to encourage their adolescents to step outside of themselves. Teenagers should look at what and who made them doubt themselves. Why did these actions affect them in a way that made them think less of themselves? What positive steps can they take to prevent this from happening again? What positive accomplishments have they already achieved to help them appreciate themselves? Teens need to remember the core value of knowing who they are and why they like and believe in themselves.

Friends

Throughout this growing-up process, especially during the pursuit of personal identities, teenagers look to their friends. Teenagers find some of their greatest stability in their friendships outside the home. These friends are the people who will listen to them, accept them for their successes and failures, support them without question, and let them mess up and not pass judgment. In short, teen friends help each other pass from childhood into adulthood. They give each other permission to try out different identities until they each find one that fits.

Quick Points

- The earliest lessons for teenagers come from observing how their parents and other care-givers behave.
- Self-exploration constitutes the first step teenagers initiate in learning who they are, what they think, how they want to live their lives, and more.
- Most teenagers get many of their strongest impressions about themselves from the media.
- The teen years and the experiences they produce involve one of the most vulnerable periods of their lives.
- Self-esteem means more than an inherent sense of self-worth. Self-esteem defines a teenager's confidence in his or her ability to think, to cope, to be happy, to feel worthy, to be entitled to assert personal needs and wants, and to enjoy the fruits of individual efforts.
- Self-esteem is something teenagers develop. No one gives it to them. They are not born with it, and it does not just happen.
- With self-esteem, teenagers can expand their choices for thoughts, actions, and reactions.
- Self-esteem provides a foundation for teenagers' trust in themselves and others.
- During their adolescence, teenagers experience mixed feelings about their independence. Sometimes, they want their parents to make decisions for them. At other times, they want their parents to leave them alone to decide for themselves.
- Adolescents normally crave independence to experiment with their own choices in matters that affect their lives.
- Adolescents will spend their teen years searching for their greatest possession: personal identity.
- Even when they generally have high self-esteem, teenagers will experience times when they do not feel so good about themselves.
- Teen friends help each other move from childhood into

adulthood by permitting each other to try out different identities until they each find one that fits.

3
Forming Friendships, Finding Groups

The radio was blaring in Alison's bedroom. She was listening to her favorite group, and tapping her pencil to the music. Alison was dividing her attention equally between the lyrics and what her best friend, Candy, was saying on the telephone. The opening of the door to Alison's personal den of privacy, which she shared only with her sister, signalled an intruder: her mother. "What do *you* want?" she clipped at her mom. "You know that I don't want you to come into this room without knocking." Respect, that's what Alison wanted. Her mother's entry had marked an intrusion, something that had been happening a lot lately, Alison thought. Candy understood Alison's dilemma and frustration, of course, because she, too, was feeling the stress of her own parents' perpetual presence in her life.

Alison and Candy demonstrate the need-package that most teenagers strive to fill. They seek respect from their parents, and private moments without the threat of parental interloping. They also want to secure trust from their parents, and encouragement to make decisions affecting their own use of time and energy. . . . Even if the ultimate activity only involves talking on the telephone in private.

Up until this time in their lives, teenagers formed their most significant impressions from watching and mimicking their parents. Their earliest experiences in relationship-building have occurred in the home, where they should. But, just as the entry into teenhood brings with it many physical changes, it also is steeped in emotional and psychological changes. In that search for identity I explained in chapter 2, we talked about the search for self. This search often requires adolescents to make a definitive separation from their parents, however trivial in action, time, or place. These initial ventures into independence serve as critical "markers" in a teenager's life. They empower teenagers to seek new definitions of themselves, separate and apart from everything that has been safe up to this point in their lives.

The Search for Privacy

During adolescence, teenagers seek ways to differentiate themselves from their parents. They seek ways to handle their lives and show signs of competence and independence.

In this search, teenagers assert themselves at home in one substantial way. They recognize and stress their ever-emerging hunger for privacy. Teenagers need privacy. It allows them to have a life of their own. Privacy also demonstrates the level of respect their parents have for them.

Respect for Privacy

Respect for privacy requires parents to keep a certain degree of distance from their teenagers. This is a difficult task for most parents, although fifty-four percent of HOBY participants said that their parents respect their preference for privacy. Eighty-seven percent believed that their siblings also respect this desire.

For respect to develop and flourish between parent and teen, parents should understand that the teen's need for privacy includes both private time and private space. Appreciating a teenager's need for privacy serves another function. It gives teenagers a sense of control within the limited parameters of their decision-making opportunities.

In the privacy of their rooms, teenagers can be alone and autonomous, and know that almost anything is possible in their private, personal domain. Teenagers use their rooms as sanctuaries, where they can exercise their independence in unobserved, unrestricted ways. Their bedrooms or other sites of sanctuary serve as places that protect teenagers from the outside world. Territory where teenagers can work out their feelings, experience pain, struggle with confusion, practice ideas, words, and behaviors. Their rooms give them space for retreat.

In their private times, teens can practice being responsible for themselves and their actions, rather than relying on their parents for every answer to every challenge they might face. However, teenagers still need to know that, even in their most private moments, their parents are available to them, to talk and to listen.

From Parents . . . to Friends

During this search for privacy, several considerations are fighting their way into the teen's consciousness. Teens might be seeking separation from their parents, but they are also seeking separation from themselves. They struggle to leave behind the child in themselves. Adolescents position themselves to emerge as adults at some unknown time in the future. They reach beyond their security zone—the home—to expand their circle of influence. Friends take on a monumental importance in teens' lives. Fortunately, according to fifty-nine percent of HOBY respondents, their parents generally approve of their friends.

> "I'm a lot like my parents and I know what kind of people will be good for me. My parents care about my well-being and they know what kind of influence I need in my life at this time."
>
> *Suzy, 15, Rural*

> "My parents generally like my friends, because they are positive influences in my life. All parents like their kids to have friends who are positive role models."
>
> *Michael, 16, Leadership*

"I haven't had any friends that my parents really dislike. I seem to choose the same type of friends that my parents would choose."

Jonathan, 17, Religious

"My mom likes all my friends, because she raised a lot of them and she loves them like they were her own kids."

Dedric, 16, Gang

Some teens, however, believe that their parents disapprove of their friendship choices, for various reasons.

"They dislike my friends, because they are gang members, and because they think I will get in a lot of trouble."

Jessie, 14, Gang

"They dislike my friends. They always criticize them for not studying enough or having lax parents, or having too much fun. I think my parents just want to protect me from bad influences."

Jenny, 16, Scholastic

Interestingly, this expansion effort is coupled with a degree of fear. Fear involves the teen's uncertainty about revealing an inner self to friends. Yet, this revelation to friends provides the very expression that helps teenagers remove their own uncertainties. Confidence in peers empowers teens to know themselves more deeply, and prepares them to be more honest with other teens who are experiencing the same insecurities. This translates into "being real" with friends in ways they might not be able to demonstrate to their own parents.

Early friendship means taking risks. Teens risk the vulnerability of exposing themselves, and all of their imperfections, to another person, a stranger. However, the miracle of friendship surfaces when teens realize that their friends are experiencing parallel fears and insecurities. Friendship translates into trust—a trust that says: "I care enough about you to be here for you, even when I might disagree with you, even when you are not your best."

The ability to make and keep friends surfaces as one of the most important growth elements teenagers develop during adolescence. Learning how to act and react sensitively to other people, which is not a birth right, requires commitment and fine-tuning throughout the remainder of their lives.

Knowing that friendship qualifies as a primary factor in their personal growth and development will give teenagers insight to help ease them through difficult times. Friendship can serve as a challenging, rewarding, and supportive force in their lives.

> "I look for friends—a group—that will listen to my problems, give me advice, and always be truthful."
> *Amber, 14, Social*

> " . . . Having good relationships, doing things after school, and getting help when you hit the rough spots."
> *Thomas, 16, Rural*

> "I expect a friend to be there for me. To feel what I feel, not because he can understand it or agree with it, but because I feel it. Then, he can tell me where I was wrong."
> *Karim, 17, Leadership*

> " . . . Someone I can be honest with, someone who won't pressure me, and someone who will loan me lunch money. A friend is someone who accepts me as I am."
> *Chris, 17, Scholastic*

Challenges to Friendship

Friendship fluctuates. It draws its definition and life from the ever-changing emotions and activities of its participants. Friendship is never completely equal or reciprocal.

No typical friendships exist. Each teenager has the capability to form friendships that have distinctive shapes and forms, through the people who define and give life to them. However, friendships do contain certain qualities that help inspire their continuity: equality, loyalty, trust, honesty, mutual respect. I will address these factors in more detail throughout the remainder of the book.

Peer Impact

When teenagers reach out, beyond their home life, to form their first extended friendships, they place themselves in positions of uncertainty. Early in the friendship process, teenagers offer and accept limited assurances and guarantees. This does not mean that teenagers intentionally avoid the qualities of friendship. Rather, they just do not know what friendship expects and demands.

Friendship offers teenagers exposure to new ways of thinking and behaving. Sometimes these changes create a kind of shock for the inexperienced teenager. This shock can produce an unexpected level of stress. This is normal, and should temper out as the adjustment process progresses.

In some ways, moving from childhood into teenhood is similar to moving to a new city or learning a new language. In many instances, the requirements of the new friendship can impose parallel demands. These and other changes in the lives of teenagers can result in a type of shock—*peer shock*. When teenagers understand why this happens, they will have an easier time with their adjustment.

Early childhood friends often defined their friendship status by proximity and timing. Children tend to seek playmates who live nearby and are available for playtime when they want to play. Teenagers, on the other hand, tend to select their friends based on interests, common beliefs, shared experiences, and more. When children socialize, they focus on a common activity. When teenagers get together, their relationships involve more complexity, and are centered around mutual trust and loyalty, as I mentioned in chapter 1. Adolescents also count on cooperation, with new lessons in the technique of give-and-take. Some teenagers learn about the giving aspects for the first time.

"I'll always be available and will do anything for my gang."

Jessie, 14, Gang

"I'm the kind of friend—member of my group—who always listens. People always tell me their troubles, their confidences. I don't have a big mouth. I'll do any favor and not expect anything in return."

Mayte, 19, Cultural

"I am a constant friend. I don't radically change my personality or actions on them. I am a loyal friend. I am there until the end, no matter what my friends and I go through. I am a fun friend. I like to be silly and light-hearted."

Mallie, 18, Leadership

Teens can also experience peer shock when their presumed friends betray or exclude them. This might occur for a variety of reasons, but often happens when loyalty is challenged. The shock of betrayal appears in many different forms. In each situation teenagers discover that, while they have been operating by one set of friendship rules, the other person has been acting out a different set of standards. This inconsistency can derive from one teen trying to gain a personal advantage in a particular situation. Or, it can be as devastating as one teen trying to change, or harm, the other teen. If this occurs, the friendship takes on a dysfunctional perspective.

Peer friendships can benefit from peer shock if these challenges to the relationship encourage or inspire teenagers to develop a stronger sense of self—a stronger personal identity and a knowingness of who they are and who they are becoming. One factor that influences the process involves teenagers' abilities to weigh the impact friends have on their decisions and actions. Teenagers, of course, must learn to accept some degree of responsibility for themselves. They should already know the difference between right and wrong. Therefore, they must accept responsibility for their actions, no matter what others try to impose on them.

The Ups and Downs of Friendship

Over the period of an extended friendship, each friend will learn to respect the other for many reasons: familiar history, common ideas, shared beliefs. At some point in every friendship, however, teenagers will probably find themselves in a rut. The commonalities they once enjoyed can lead friends into unexpected territory: the land of boredom and superficiality.

This stagnant, unrewarding stage of friendship—which one friend is often more sensitive to than the other—can lead to a serious imbalance. If not honestly addressed by both friends, this imbalance can destroy their friendship. For example, if one teen dominates as the giver in the friendship, with the other teen being a constant taker, the relationship will probably self-destruct. Balance and freshness need to prevail in healthy friendships.

In most instances, when friends have problems between them, they need to commit to conflict resolution. By ignoring problems, friends challenge the strength of their intimate bond. Fortunately, when difficulties with impact do arise, solid friendships usually endure.

> "At this time in my life, friendship means: someone to talk to and share my feelings with, someone to spend good quality time with, and someone to turn to when I need help."
>
> *Tera, 16, Religious*

> "Friendship has taken on a more emotional aspect. There's less emphasis placed on hanging out, doing things together, and sharing stories. Now there's more emphasis on helping one another through emotionally trying situations."
>
> *Karim, 17, Leadership*

> "Friendship used to mean having someone to play with on the playground, but now it means having someone to depend on and someone who depends on you."
>
> *LiAn, 16, Scholastic*

Adolescents find it easier to forgive a friend's behavior than almost anyone else's, even when it is serious and sometimes has a negative effect. After all, don't friends stick up for each other?

Some friends do better than others at accepting advice. Teenagers should be careful to give peer counsel only when they truly believe that they can share beneficial insight with their friends. Good friends must be willing to put sensitivities on the line for the sake of the greater friendship and ultimate welfare of their friends.

Other friendship challenges teens face revolve around finding faults in their friends, when those faults actually lie within themselves. Sometimes this occurs when teenagers misread their own needs or those of their friends. For example, many teenagers assume that when a friend shares insight with them they should offer advice. Not true. An effective total communicator would listen and respect the friend's feelings. This means that when a teenager opens up emotionally, sharing a very personal story with a friend, the friend should absorb the words and the emotions of the message. This also means that the listening friend must avoid interruptions and personal comparisons. Just offering a listener's ear can be one of the greatest gifts friends can give to each other. In the same regard, friends should not insensitively impose their needs on one another, nor totally disregard the potential or actual responses of their listening friends.

Resolving Conflict

When conflict, however complex, arises in friendship, both friends need to seek resolution as soon as possible. By letting tempers simmer or misunderstandings brew, friends test their friendship in unhealthy, preventable ways.

Teenagers also need to realize that they have the right not to agree with their friends. A crucial part of friendship involves recognizing the differences—as often as the likenesses—that drew them together in the first place . . . especially when they are handling conflict. By resolving conflict, friends do not need to determine a right and wrong person or point-of-view. Such resolution requires each friend to honestly share information with the other. It also compels each friend to resolve the problem. Solid friendships reinforce these opportunities, and the growth of the friendship that results.

> " . . . From sharing toys to counseling crises. As a teenager, most of my friendships are now formed with the purpose of consulting in a crisis situation."
>
> *Michael, 16, Leadership*

> "I hang out with them a lot more, and I think it's harder to keep friends than when you were a little kid. Tough times require tough actions."
>
> *Jason, 17, Gang*

> "Friends used to be people to play with. Now they're special people who grow up with you . . . even with all of the hang-ups you might have between you."
>
> *Chris, 17, Wrestler*

A powerful way to confront conflict incorporates a four-part communication formula. The "when you-I feel-because-I prefer" approach to conflict resolution helps teens in tough times.

> "*When you* . . . " The teen states a particular disturbing behavior. For example, "When you decide what we're going to do on a Friday night without asking me . . . "
> "*I feel* . . . " The teen specifies an emotional response. "I feel disappointed and cheated."
> "*Because* . . ." The teen describes in enough detail why this action arouses these particular feelings. "Because you choose activities that I often do not enjoy."
> "*I prefer* . . ." The teen explains a preferred replacement behavior that the friend should adopt. "I prefer that you include me in the planning, so that I know my ideas and interests are important to you."

Accountability

The bonds of friendship thrive on a sense of generosity and mutuality. Friends are givers, listeners, and respecters. Friendship does not take form in terms of wins and losses. It does, however, require accountability. When teenagers realize that they must think and act accountably, they realize that they are involved in an active process. They recognize that they have options as well as the ability to act on their choices for action.

Therefore, teenagers who practice friendship honestly do not blame others for what happens to them. They do not get angry at their parents for not doing for them what they can do for themselves. They do not expect things to "just happen." Yes, even in the best of times, teenagers—like adults—"slip" and blame others, just to relieve themselves from the pressures that making mistakes imposes. However, this finger-pointing does not solve any issues.

Friendship practitioners know that they have the ability to make things happen. Responsible adolescents realize that when they act and react accountably, someone—even if it is only themselves—has placed trust in them to see it through. By being honest with themselves first, adolescents learn to count on themselves first. This reduces the pressure of counting on their friends to solve their problems—often an impossible task, anyway.

Forgiving Friends

When teen friends disappoint each other, bruised emotions often result. When friends store mental junk about each other, it can place stumbling blocks in the way of the friendship. To resolve and recover, friends need to learn the art and skill of *forgiveness*.

Deciding to forgive a friend is a choice. Other choices include anger and disappointment. When teenagers select negative options, the friendship can suffer. By choosing to forgive, friends replace the desire to hold on to anger with the greater desire to maintain an important friendship bond. By preferring to forgive, teens put aside pride, admit they have done something—however slight—that is wrong or improper, and become willing to move forward with the friendship.

Another antagonist that can stand in the way of forgiveness is *guilt*. Real guilt—for real errors—has the power, however, to provide positive results. It can challenge teenagers to *seek* forgiveness. Unfortunately, guilt most often prompts teenagers to stand in their own way. It creates a reluctance within teens to forgive themselves. Therefore, in dealing with forgiveness, teenagers should:

- Forgive friends and learn to forgive themselves first.
- Carefully evaluate lofty expectations and standards, and consider whether they are expecting too much of themselves and others.
- Shed the form of guilt that serves as a patterned response to life itself.
- Forgive themselves, and believe in themselves, without the entanglement of unnecessary guilt.
- Set aside ill feelings about themselves and others, and be willing to act in spite of those potentially debilitating feelings.
- Act now, rather than wait for the right opportunity to offer forgiveness to themselves and others.

Balancing Friendship with Honesty

Teenagers live extraordinarily busy lives. This results, in part, from the jet-tracking explained in chapter 1. It also occurs as a result of the complexities that growing up demands of teenagers.

However affected by outside influences, teenagers must exercise honesty for their friendships to survive and surpass. When a teenager deceives a friend, this action can damage the friendship itself. When friends disagree or hurt each other's feelings, they need to reassure each other of their basic caring and concern, the foundation of their friendship.

Even in the earliest stages, honesty counts. Teens need to

determine early how willingly and honestly they will contribute to the friendship. It starts with a teenager's basic acceptance of the friend as an individual, a person with a distinctive identity. Honesty helps friends assure each other that they can accept one another. It helps them assist each other with their forward-moving process of becoming adults.

Honesty plays an even more significant role in keeping friends than in the initial start-up of the friendship. It provides the foundation for reciprocity. Teenagers should recognize and accept that the friendship will thrive only when each friend benefits. Honesty serves as a stabilizer through good times and bad times, both of which can challenge the friendship itself.

Honesty underscores the communication between friends. This means when teenagers speak, and when they listen. It affects the communication that occurs within each teenager, in the private moments when friendship can have its most important presence.

Expanding from One Friend to the Group

As I have explained in this chapter, each friendship has its own quality, its own distinctiveness. Some friendships are private, one-to-one. They sustain themselves because the two people involved have a special connection that others—outsiders—cannot penetrate.

Other friendships occur in a broader sense, and exist only when the people are involved and active in a larger circle of people. These friendships exist within a complex network, or networks, of friendships. As I mentioned in the preface, *one plus one* equals the beginning of a group. One plus one can create the invitation for an interconnectedness with others who have separate friendships. As teenagers constantly seek new definitions of who they are, they are also experiencing a transition that affects the way they select their friends. These expanded identities help teenagers explore new frontiers of friendship—the Group.

Quick Points

- Teenagers seek out privacy to differentiate themselves from their parents.
- Privacy gives teenagers the opportunity to exercise their independence.
- In their early searches for independence from their parents, teenagers experience a degree of uncertainty and fear.
- Early friendship requires risk-taking.
- Friendship always fluctuates.
- Friendship offers teenagers exposure to new ways of thinking and acting.
- Requirements imposed by new friendships create stress for teenagers. This can result in *peer shock*.
- Peer shock often results from change itself, or from perceived betrayal, or from many other experiences that the teenager has never known before.
- Teenagers can experience ruts in their friendships that can lead to imbalances in the friendship.
- Balance and freshness need to prevail in healthy friendships.
- Teenagers must excel as two-way communicators in their friendships: listeners as well as speakers.
- When conflicts arise, teenagers need to resolve them as soon as possible.
- A powerful way to deal with disturbing behavior with a friend is to adopt the "When You-I Feel-Because-I Prefer" Formula.
- The bond of friendship thrives on a sense of generosity and mutuality.
- Teenagers need to recognize their own accountability in the friendship process.
- Healthy friendships include the art and skill of forgiveness.
- Teenagers must make a commitment to honesty for their friendships to survive and surpass.
- Some friendships are private. Others thrive in a larger circle of friends.

- As teenagers constantly redefine their identities, they also move into new ways to select their friends. They explore new frontiers of friendship—the Group.

4
Peer Impact
From Recruitment to Refuge

Larry entered the heavy metal doors of his new school. He looked down a hallway that seemed to run the length of two football fields, with no end in sight (an apt observation for Larry, as this hallway symbolized his innermost feelings and needs). The first day of school filled him with hopes and promises for new friends and newfound experiences. "It all starts here, and now," he told himself. To belong, to be accepted by others: one step forward into the hallway of miles, a definitive first step in the process of group membership.

It does not take entering a new school to define the progress from single friendships to group membership. In fact, for the purposes of this book, I have defined a *group* as *two or more individuals who are assembled together and/or have a unifying relationship*. This means that early relationships between children and their first "best friends" contribute substantial know-how to teenagers when they begin to experience their first group involvement. One plus one, as I said in the preface, equals the beginning of a group.

In their teen years, most youths experience a special need for membership in groups. So how do teens and groups connect? How does the selection process begin? How do groups seek out new members? When does the *recruitment* process begin?

Recruitment

In many groups, recruitment is obvious. Existing members actively seek out potential members and encourage them to join. For example, high school service clubs might have "rush" parties, where they entertain and promote themselves and their club to potential peer members. Once they decide to join, these members might be welcomed at an initiation dinner or event.

Another example is the Junior ROTC. Natasha Morrison, ROTC Cadet of the Year in her high school in Honolulu, joined the program, because it encouraged her to develop her own potential. Many high schoolers who join this group experience their first official commitment to a program. Though this commitment mandates specific requirements of membership, many of the participants consider the process a plus. It gives them a chance to get to know and respect each other. They also have the opportunity to build their self-esteem and do something positive with their lives.

At the other extreme, gangs often travel to other cities and states to recruit their members. These recruits are often preadolescents, young people with high susceptibility to joining. Once accepted, rather than being the participants in an official event, these recruits are "jumped in"—beat up by several gang members.

Before taking on a group identity—before being recruited into group membership—teenagers should consider how a particular group will work and answer several personal needs. Teenagers have a right to seek a group that will:

- Have people they can trust and want to call their friends. Teens should ask: Will this group help me meet people I want to know and spend time with?
- Provide opportunities. Teens should ask: Will I be able to share my interests, while learning new and useful things when I belong to this group?
- Give them lasting reasons for staying in the group. Teens should ask: Will I grow and become a better person because of my ongoing membership in this group?

- Equip them with tools to deal with different situations and different people in different environments. Teens should ask: Will I learn how to interact effectively with other group members, even when we do not always agree?
- Balance the needs of the individual with the needs of the group. Teens should ask: Will the group move forward with its own purpose, and still respect my personal needs for growth and individuality?
- Inspire them to make contributions. Teens should ask: Will my being a member of this group empower me to make a difference in this group and elsewhere?

When teenagers venture into groups for the first time, they often must say good-bye to their old friends to welcome the new ones. This can be a difficult choice for teenagers. Old friends provide a level of comfort. Teenagers have learned to count on them. They have shared a common history that has provided a sense of stability and security. These were the first peers who accepted them with all of the strengths and weaknesses that comprised personal identity. Old friends serve as measuring sticks for a teen's progress. They are the people who knew the teen when. . . .

Old friends, however, reinforce the sense of history and struggle that teens often want to leave behind. Just like Larry entering his school for the first time, many teenagers want to "begin over" in a new environment. In a new setting, many teenagers see a world of possibilities, with no prior imprints in concrete to distract them.

Of course, new friends and group membership do not require drastic moves into new environments. Sometimes, change only involves the mere exchange of one friend for another. Or the evolutionary step from a single friend into a group. With group membership comes the expansion of the friendship circle and the safety of numbers. Whatever the chosen route, this movement helps define a process of self-discovery for teenagers. Through this process adolescents can present themselves as they are becoming, not as they have been.

A Different Look at Belonging

An important part of the growth process, in particular the movement into a group, includes selecting people who will enhance and expand the personal development experience. Teenagers should not limit themselves only to those people who mirror their own identities. These likenesses might be physical, intellectual, or emotional.

"I expect my close friends to have my same ideals, but I have learned to accept those who don't."

Kristy, 17, Religious

"I want to respect others and I want others to respect me, and each of us to set good examples for the other."

Kiki, 14, Gang

Cliques

In the early stages of group selection, teenagers might hazard their experiences by seeking out people in a "clique" rather than developing more honest group membership. How does a clique impair personal development for teenagers?

Cliques use their power to hurt and/or to manipulate people. Anthony Wolf, in his book, *Get Out of My Life* (The Noonday Press, 1991), considers the purpose of the clique to give each member a sense of self-worth, which is "inextricably tied to the exclusiveness of the clique." He adds, "A clique can serve its purpose only by being a clique, by excluding others, by putting them down."

"I'm popular, or so people say. I hang out with all kinds of people, but the 'clique' is who I feel at home with. My clique is very selective about where we go and where we're seen. I like the closeness of it, even though it's kind of fake."

Lisa, 16, Leadership

"When I first started in my group, it included everyone. Now it's a few select people. This can be good and bad."

Erika, 18, Employment

"I don't associate with people outside my group, because of the differences and point-of-views in our lives."

Tera, 16, Religious

"This depends on the group. If the group is closed to outsiders, it might make you cold to others. If it is open and inviting to others, you will be, too."

Paul, 19, Cultural

For boys, popularity and cliques represent a step in growing up. Prior to adolescence, boys consider sports and "toughness" the measures of success. In their teen years, boys learn that "hanging out" with their friends can be a favorite activity. These emerging alliances, however, can prompt a new level of "competition."

In her book, *But Everyone Else Looks So Sure* (Shoe Tree Press, 1991), author Denise V. Long describes girls' cliques as "those that tend to focus on manipulating friendships and feelings." Cliques can take on an extraordinary purpose for young teenage girls seeking popularity. Fortunately, as she progresses into the later years of adolescence, the average teenage girl will distinguish the difference between being popular and finding friendship.

"I don't see myself as popular. I see myself as a person with a lot of friends from several different groups."

Amber, 14, Social

"I'm friends with people from all groups. I don't see myself as popular but more as friendly. I spend time with my horse-lover friends, because of our same interests."

Suzy, 15, Rural

"I am not popular. I belong to just a few groups. I spend the most time with friends that I have grown up and gone to school with. I like being with them because they understand my point of view and usually agree with me."

Mallie, 18, Leadership

Cliques tend to reject and hurt their members and other people, rather than promote positive relationships and activities inside and outside their group. This definition, therefore, qualifies gangs, cults, and other antisocial groups as cliques more than most other friendship groups on the teen scene.

"I belong to one group, and we spend our time by kickin' it with my 'homeboys' at a party or at the lake all night with some 40's (40-ounce-beers)."

Jessie, 14, Gang

"I hang around with one group, because the other groups are kinda gang cliques, and I'm definitely an outsider."

Justin, 14, Rural

"I tend to hang out with the 'bad' crowd more, because those people usually understand me and my problems better."

Jennifer, 16, Social

No Groups

Another consideration about group identities includes those people who do not belong to a group at all. Some teenagers decide not to participate in groups, because they prefer their solitude, or they cannot find a group that satisfies their needs. Sometimes they avoid joining groups, because they are rebelling, and this helps them deny what is expected.

Other teens are *non*members of groups, because no particular groups accept them. This can create painful feelings in teenagers who are treated as outsiders. Some teenagers respond to this situation by creating new avenues for associations with others. They also might look to diversity, rather than similarity, as a criterion for friendship-selection. This encourages opportunities for inclusion rather than exclusion. A good example of this is Green Circle, a program that helps preteens learn to develop self-esteem, gain awareness of other groups, and resolve conflicts peacefully. This program, located in northern California, teaches students that it is all right to care and share with people who are unlike themselves. Teenagers from other groups agree:

"Everyone should be friends with everyone."

Stephanie, 14, Social

"In my neighborhood I just have to stick to my own. My group helps me go beyond this . . . to meet other people from all races and cultures, and to make friends with people unlike me."

Mayte, 19, Cultural

"People who are not members of my group are carefully examined and tested before they are accepted. This type of treatment bugs me, and I try to be more open."

Jonathan, 17, Religious

Multigroup Membership

Other teenagers prefer not to belong to just one group, because this limits their choices. Multigroup membership also prevents teenagers from getting too narrowly focused in their interests and their selection of friends.

"I spend a lot of time in many different groups. I usually hang around with well put-together, intelligent, popular people."

Joshua, 17, Social

"I do have many friends who like me. I hang around with many people. I like to get involved with whatever or whomever I can."

Charla, 15, SADD

"I 'belong' to several groups. I spend the most time with the group that I have known for a long period of time, because we know how each of us feels about important things."

Kassi, 14, Rural

Without multigroup memberships, many teenagers experience the sting of being labeled or stereotyped. This can be very difficult for teens at this stage of life.

> "I feel I'm stereotyped. Some Hispanic friends don't feel like they belong to my group so they criticize me for being in it. They say that I'm in it to feel accepted."
>
> *Xochitl, 20, Cultural*

> "The group I'm in sets us apart from others in almost everything we do at school. I want to believe that this disadvantage is outweighed by the long-term advantages."
>
> *Jasmine, 16, Scholastic*

The Search for Peer Approval

One of the greatest pursuits for teenagers is that of *peer approval*. Teen agendas focus on their drive to be accepted, and to look appropriate to those people they want to impress—their peers. A teen's peers can include equals, friends, other kids they know, or just kids in general.

As teenagers separate from their parents, they hungrily search for friends—groups—who welcome them and offer a ready support system. To teenagers, this often represents their first independent experience with the outside world. So, success at this level can be extremely important to them.

Peer pressure means being influenced, convinced, or talked into doing or not doing something by friends. The matter of "pressure" implies, at least in some instances, that the teenagers are being forced in a way that goes against their true feelings or values. Groups often pressure their members to conform to the group's ideas and desires. This sometimes might diverge from the individual teenager's ideas or wishes. Often, this pressure occurs with risk-taking behaviors like smoking, drinking, drugs, and sexual relations.

Parents regularly experience an equally disturbing struggle during their children's emergence into peer relationship-building. Parents worry about their teens' choice of friends. They concern themselves that "bad" influences will prevail in their teens' lives. They fret that their children will make the wrong friends, and do the wrong things. These and similar concerns often prompt battles between parents and teens, and can create unnecessary ill feelings. Ironically selecting friends helps teenagers learn how to deal with all kinds of people, and diverse relationships.

"My parent only asks that my friends be honest and not ex-convicts."

Alyssa, 15, Letterman

"My mother wants me to pick new friends all the time. This is not because she doesn't like the ones I have, but because she wants me to have a selection or variety. She has never forced me to be a friend to any particular person or join any particular group."

Mary, 16, SADD

"My parents tend to evaluate my friends. However, when I evaluate theirs they are offended. They want my friends to be honorable.

Michael, 16, Leadership

"They don't influence whom I pick as friends, and they don't tell me how my friends should act. If they did, I would have a serious talk with them."

Natalie, 17, Choir

"My parents don't want my friends to be gang members. They want them to be good friends who don't get in trouble."

Jessie, 14, Gang

"My mom really doesn't tell me what she wants my friends to be like, just as long as they don't get me in any more trouble than usual."

Jennifer, 16, Social

Dealing with Negative Peer Pressure

The 1994-95 *USA Today* Teen Panel (*USA Today*, August 19, 1994) considers peer pressure a force that can push teenagers in all directions. Fifteen-year-old Alexandra Perakis, of Wilton, Connecticut, admitted that her friends "influence me on almost everything I do. I am extremely worried about people's opinions and feel the need to fit in."

To deal with negative peer pressure teenagers need to recognize their own self-worth. They should realize that *self-acceptance* is one of the most important elements of their personal growth and empowerment. This does not mean other people's approval, consent, permission, agreement, sympathy, support. . . . It does signify that teenagers should learn to accept themselves. They need to acknowledge that the way things are can be okay. It means that teenagers learn to accept their lives at the "now" stage so that they can move forward in a healthy way to the "what's next" stage of their personal development. Only then can teenagers propel themselves from inaction to productive action. Through self-acceptance, teenagers can relax and find patience and strength to move forward.

Jeff was a sprinter on his high school track team. He had lettered and had set several zone records. In his senior year, a new coach was hired to replace the one who had trained Jeff for three years. At first, Jeff was upset. His teammates were unhappy, too. They continually urged Jeff to quit the team. They said he wouldn't be a star under the new coach, and should not waste his time going to practice. Jeff really struggled with the situation. He felt cheated. He was angry, because he believed what his teammates said. He decided to quit the team, but thought he should tell the coach why. During his conversation with the coach, he learned about the coach's plans to put him on the first team. The coach also explained how he would help the team through the transition and respect their input. Jeff changed his mind, and stayed on the team. To his surprise, Jeff did run in events throughout the season and excelled at the sport.

Self-acceptance is evolutionary. By accepting their experiences and relationships for what they are, and how they can contribute to personal development, teenagers can turn this knowledge into learning experiences. These lessons can empower teenagers to avoid negative peer pressure, and to excel in personal development.

Another way of dealing with negative peer pressure encourages teenagers to think ahead. They should ask themselves:

- What might happen if I give in by doing or not doing something that the group is pressing me about?
- What might happen if I do not succumb to peer pressure?
- How will I feel about myself afterward?
- What can I expect from other people if I do or do not give in to peer pressure?
- Could I get into trouble if I do what the group is pressing me to do or not to do?
- Am I willing to "pay the price" for listening to and acting the way the group wants me to act?

A third alternative to negative peer pressure involves *talking honestly about feelings* and inviting others to do the same. Teenagers who assert themselves are often surprised that many of their friends have the same hesitations about peer pressure. Open dialogue can work wonders in helping them resolve their dilemmas.

Humor and *overstatement* provide other alternatives for battling negative peer pressure. For example, teenagers can challenge what they consider to be an unwise activity by saying: "Are you crazy, that's one of the dumbest ideas I ever heard." If the activity is immoral, the teen might say: "Only a low-life would do something like that." If the activity poses an element of uncertainty, an optional response might be: "This is a tough decision. It makes me feel like I have to choose between taking a million dollars and getting my degree without going to college."

A sixth choice involves *using parents as a reason*. "My parents would put me on restriction for the rest of my life" goes a long way in fending off negative peer pressure.

Teenagers have yet another option: *Just say "no."* This might actually be the most difficult word they will have to use, but it also might be the most important one.

Not-So-Negative, Really

Before presuming the worst, most peer groups give positive choices to their members. Sports, academics, leadership, community service, professional development. In fact, many teens recognize that peer pressure can be positive. Members of the 1994-95 *USA Today* Teen Panel agreed that peer pressure has a variable impact. Seventeen-year-old Benny Hsu, of Jacksonville, Florida, said, "I used to be shy, but my friends persuaded me to be open to good change."

Other teen panelists said that peer pressure is overrated. Seventeen-year-old Angela Paradise, of Indianapolis, Indiana, said, "I fail to believe peer pressure is as widespread as it is depicted. It seems it has become more of a cop-out, a scapegoat, than a real thing."

"It's a ready excuse for our shortcomings and failures. Sometimes, but not always, I think the phrase serves as an easy excuse for not having the guts to stand up for what we believe in," added sixteen-year-old Lisa LaBrecque, of Westfield, Massachusetts.

Peer pressure might play a more powerful role in the development and need for acceptance by younger teens. "In junior high school, your friends made absolutely every decision in your life," according to fourteen-year-old Eddie Jurken III, of Brookfield, Wisconsin. "I'm not saying that friends don't influence you in high school, but they certainly don't control you."

Other teenagers on the panel said they succumb to peer pressure only on little matters, like after-school activities. When it comes to the big issues, teens said self-esteem is the strongest weapon in fighting negative peer pressure. "People who have low self-esteem will do pretty much anything their peers tell them in order to be accepted," said fourteen-year-old Melissa Wood, of Virginia Beach, Virginia.

However, teen growth requires a healthy involvement with people who can offer other teen members of the group diversity of thought, attitude, experience, and action. Membership cloning has the potential to stunt individual development. Teens need to weigh the opinions, ideas, and actions of their group. Most teenagers already know this. Sixty-two percent of HOBY respondents said that they only "sometimes" let other people influence their own thinking and actions.

Peer Influence, Now and Later

Yes, peer groups do provide reasons for parental concern. Especially when parents realize that their teens are so committed to finding approval from their peers.

Peer groups do not sustain their power indefinitely over the vast majority of teen-members. As teenagers develop their own identities and progress into adulthood, the role of their teen groups tends to diminish. Adolescents usually keep the friendships that work, whether or not the group remains important to them. And they find new groups to join as their interests and needs evolve.

Refuge: Group Safety

One of the primary reasons for teen membership in groups centers around *safety*. Teenagers seek the comfort of others and the protections they offer. The teen years provide enough turbulence. At least friends should be able to help them survive.

Personal Safety Zones Offer Protection

In the search, teenagers look for personal *safety zones*. A safety zone can be any place or activity—mental or physical—that gives teenagers comfort and a sense of security. This can be a basketball court, a room, a favorite hang-out, studying a favorite subject, attending an aerobics class, or talking on the telephone with a friend. Teenagers test their safety zones when they do something new or different.

For teenagers to grow, they need to challenge their safety zones. Otherwise, their safety zones will actually shrink and disappear. To ensure that the safety zone survives, the teenager will need to overcome fears of the unknown and the undone. This, of course, requires venturing beyond what is comfortable, to experience new and different things—those that teenagers might otherwise be afraid to do. Or . . . might think they are unable to accomplish. By moving beyond safety zones, teenagers might not like everything they try. That's okay. The effort alone will help them discover answers and solutions they might not have sought if they had continued to wrap themselves up in the warmth and security of their individual safety zone.

Groups often provide teenagers with the insulation of a safety zone. The support of friends, and the comfort they provide, reassures teenagers that they are welcome and have people—the group—to take them in and shelter them from the outside.

Shebon discovered the truth of this principle when she tried out for a school play. She had never performed in public before, and had felt uncomfortable with the idea of looking foolish in front of her friends. So Shebon did other things that were easier for her—the school newspaper and band. A few of her classmates who belonged to the drama club encouraged her to audition for the lead. She did not get the part. However, she did join the drama club and developed a new appreciation for theater. In addition to belonging to a group that supported her, Shebon also developed an interest in theater as a set designer.

Of course, teenagers usually will know, too, when they are involved with the wrong group—for them, anyway. This often occurs when they find themselves wanting to "get away" from the group, when they would rather be almost anywhere else, doing anything else, rather than spending time with these people.

The Need for Safety Starts with Parents

What teenagers learn about safety zones they often learn from their parents, by observing what their parents do to create safety and comfort for themselves. Parents, teachers, and other adults play an instrumental role in establishing boundaries for teenagers. They set the rules for what teenagers can and cannot do, with whom, and when. Most often, too, they base their intentions on concern for the teen's safety and protection. For example, teenagers are expected to follow curfew, whether determined by the law or their parents. This time-to-be-home rule usually reflects the parents' need to protect their teenagers by making sure that they are home during the high-risk times of the night.

> "My parents encourage my activities with sports, scouts, and school. I need to get home by 9 PM on school nights, and by 11 PM on weekends. And, they're strict about no 'one-on-one.'"
>
> *Thomas, 16, Rural*

> "My parents want the chance to veto my choice of activities. They don't like me to spend large amounts of time away from home with my friends."
>
> *Jonathan, 17, Religious*

Parents often determine other rules with and for their teenagers, many of which directly or indirectly involve safety.

> "The kinds of rules my mom wants me to follow are to come in the house when something is about to happen, and do my chores before I go to hang with my friends."
>
> *Dedric, 16, Gang*

> "My mother has never set any rules except for being home by midnight. I think she assumes that no drugs and not getting arrested go without saying."
>
> *Jasmine, 16, Scholastic*

"I am really free to do what I want as long as I can keep on top of my responsibilities. If I don't keep on top of my responsibilities then I get burned in school, work or whatever. That has been pretty good discipline."

Karim, 17, Leadership

Safety Zones Have Growth Potential

As teenagers expand the dimensions of their safety zones, they will be able to develop more power and control over their lives. At the same time, they will naturally test their safety zones, to experiment with the "outside." Groups play a significant role in a teenager's outreach.

Groups have the ability to substitute a new source of security for that safety the teenager enjoyed at home. The members of a group provide nurturing and support to help fill the void its teenage members might experience while testing their personal safety zones. During this pursuit for new experiences, adolescents learn about their potential, and learn to define what is important to them. Also, with the assistance and often encouragement of the group, they learn which risks are worthwhile in their efforts to excel.

Quick Points

- A *group* is defined as *two or more individuals who are assembled together and/or have a unifying relationship.*
- Recruitment of teenagers for membership in a group will vary from group to group.
- Before joining a group, teenagers should consider how a particular group will work.
- Teenagers have a right to seek a group based on several criteria. They should ask:
  - Does the group have people I can trust and will want to call friends?
  - Will group membership provide opportunities?
  - Will the group give me lasting reasons for staying in the group?

- Will the group help me deal with different situations and different people in different environments?
- Will the group balance my needs with the needs of the group?
- Will the group inspire me to make contributions?

- The venture into groups often requires a teenager to say good-bye to old friends.
- Old friends represent a source of security for teenagers, while new friends and groups often provide a sense of adventure.
- In selecting groups, teenagers should consider picking friends who are not mere replicas of themselves.
- When joining a group, teenagers should consider how the group will affect their personal development process.
- *Cliques* generally use their power in negative ways, not necessarily considering the needs of the individual.
- Some teenagers avoid group membership because they prefer solitude, or cannot find the right group, or are rejected. Some just prefer to belong to more than one circle of friends.
- One of a teenager's greatest searches is for *peer approval*.
- As teenagers separate from their parents, they turn to their friends—groups—for their support system.
- *Peer pressure* means being influenced, convinced, or talked into doing or not doing something by friends.
- Parents are often concerned that their teenagers will select friends who are "bad influences" on their children.
- To confront negative peer pressure teenagers should recognize their own self-worth.
- Self-acceptance is evolutionary.
- Ways for teenagers to handle peer pressure include: thinking ahead, talking honestly about their feelings, employing humor and overstatement, using their parents as a reason for their decision, and saying "No" even when it is difficult.
- Many teenagers think the idea of peer pressure is overrated, and might be more influential for younger teenagers than older ones.

- Peer influence often fades away as teenagers establish and feel comfortable with their emerging adult identities.
- One of the primary reasons for group membership centers around *safety*. Teenagers seek the comfort of others—outside the home—and the protections they provide.
- Teenagers search for personal *safety zones*. Groups often provide teenagers with the insulation of a safety zone.
- For teenagers to grow, they need to challenge their safety zones.
- As teenagers expand the dimensions of their safety zones, they will develop more power and control over their lives.

5
The Merging Process

The marquee held larger-than-life block letters, spelling out the movie title, *The Crow*. Already a legend, the film had become a first-choice event for Stephanie and her friends. Again, for the third time in two weeks, the group of teenagers energetically exited the movie theater, prepared to move on to their next shared activity. This is the way they did things— together. Friends since the first year of high school, the girls were almost inseparable. They got their hair cut by the same stylist, traded clothes on a regular basis, spent every spare moment with each other, exchanged language and ideas like trade secrets, and put everyone else second. After all, they were the group—best friends for life.

When teenagers move into the group-friendship stage of their lives, they often move into a process of *merging* with their friends. In some ways, they become interchangeable with each other. They see themselves in each other and cling to these mirrored images of themselves. The reflection provides a source of security. It also provides opportunities to team with friends to share ideas, experiences, emotions, and other parts of growing up with people like them: the group.

As teenagers begin this merging process, they discover more and more about what they have in common with the group. In chapter 1, I explained the weight that teenagers give to trust, loyalty, and commitment. Another significant factor for teenagers, as they merge and emerge, is *mutuality*. Teenagers seek out people with whom they can share their time, interests, ideas, attitudes, and more.

Through the adolescent years, a teenager might have hundreds of acquaintances. The number of friends will total only a minute fraction of that, possibly only a handful. One reason for this centers around the ways teenagers recognize and appreciate the values they share between them. This helps them enjoy a better sense of togetherness and purpose. Once teenagers have established this bond, they demonstrate their union in many ways.

Clothing, Symbols, and Music

Teenage groups adopt certain distinctive symbols to describe who they are and why they are different from others. One way to accomplish this identity is through clothing. Teenagers today are more vocal than ever about what they will and will not wear. While one group might wear the "seventies retro look," another group might wear jeans and oversized tee-shirts. Still another group might identify itself from outsiders through jewelry, such as pins, necklaces, earrings, and bracelets, or with accessories like belts, hats, and sunglasses. Even haircuts and gestures distinguish groups. On the more permanent level, some groups make their membership with "body art" that can involve tattooing, piercing, and even branding.

> "These 'signs' are important so you know just by looking at someone what they are into."
>
> *Chris, 17, Wrestler*

> "We know who we are, because of our blue rags, hair nets, and the way we wear our pants."
>
> *Jeremy, 17, Gang*

> "In 4-H we wear green ties, white shirts, and dark or black jeans. It shows people that we are with the 4-H, and gives them good impressions."
>
> *Cara, 15, Rural*

Some teens prefer not to draw attention to their group membership.

> "There don't have to be any visual signs or symbols to show you are part of a group. If that's all you care about, you're in for the wrong reasons."
>
> *Neil, 17, Leadership*

> "I think it's okay to greet people of your group in your special way. But when it turns to killing, like gang signs, that's obviously not a good idea. Our group's 'sign' is probably wearing our Texas Instruments-82 calculators."
>
> *Jasmine, 16, Scholastic*

Language

Language serves as another identifying factor in and for the group. As children move into adolescence, their language will take on a new life—that of their peers, their group. In fact, language can take on its own degree of "secrecy" as the teens learn to create an exclusivity with their intragroup communications.

> "It's important that we speak our own language to each other and share our common goals and cultures."
>
> *Africa, 19, Cultural*

> "I will talk Spanish with them."
>
> *Jessie, 14, Gang*

> "I tend to adapt, yet I never dishonor my code of conduct. Every group has slang and, in order to be part of a group, the ability to adapt is a must."
>
> *Michael, 16, Leadership*

Some teens want to avoid isolating themselves in such overt ways.

"If I took on the ideas, slang, and attitudes of a group, then I'd lose my own sense of who I am."

Chris, 17, Wrestler

"Keeping your own identity is a big thing. Having someone else's is stupid."

Stephanie, 14, Social

"I am willing to take on a group's ideas and attitudes if they are similar to mine, but I will not take on the ideas and attitudes if they change what I really feel."

LiAn, 16, Scholastic

Slang Mirrors the Times

Teenagers usually have the flexibility and ease to adopt the language of the moment. For example, during the O.J. Simpson trial in 1995, hip-hop generation teenagers adopted the expression, "O.J.," which took on the meaning: To beat up, as in a domestic dispute. In the same vein, O.J. Simpson's attorney, Robert Shapiro, was immortalized by the creation of a verb in his name: to shapiro. This means to convince somebody.

In gang groups, or as I mentioned in chapter 4—better described as cliques—language plays a crucial role. It aligns the members of the gang, more so than in most other groups. Gang language also alienates outsiders. These words or expressions will vary from region to region. A sample of the expressions I learned during my research with gang members for this book include:

Chillin' in the cut: Hanging around the house.
Cud: Marijuana.
Dank (Sherm Stick): Filterless cigarette dunked in embalming fluid. Produces effects similar to angel dust.
Doing dirt (punishments): Hurting or shooting someone.
Family: The order of hierarchy within a gang.
Got my back: Looking after a fellow gang member.

Homeboy: Fellow gang buddy.

Jumped into a gang: To get into a gang, the initiate must go into a room with six to eight gang members who beat him or her up.

Kickin' it: Hanging out with gang members.

Runs: Dope runs, beer runs, drive-by shootings.

Traveling times: Time it takes to get drugs; time to leave.

Language Means More than Words

Interestingly, language can involve more than just words and phrases. The language of friendship within the group expands to the communication of concern and caring for each other. The actions and confidences that friends share comprise the "words" of the friendship. Teenagers can expand their friendships by vocalizing these words. Often, though, they share their communication through action, and attitude, without the spoken word. HOBY participants identified the global significance of this language.

"A friend shares herself with you through understanding, consideration, and tolerance."

Girl, 15, Great Britain

"Friends believe in you and encourage you to believe in them just as much."

Boy, 16, Japan

"To me, a friend shows interest in you, your feelings, your hopes, and your dreams."

Girl, 15, USA

For many teenagers, even opportunity to talk with each other on the telephone gives them the chance to refine and reinforce their language regularly. They can freely exchange their ideas and expressions, without the involvement and interference of outsiders. Each telephone dialogue provides the focused setting for reinforcing the vocabulary of the group, while solidifying it in other ways as well.

Shared Interests, Activities

When teenagers share interests—when they like the same things—they have taken a giant step toward building friendship in their group. When teenagers look for friendships, they often search for common interests first. For the shared interest to provide staying power for group members, however, their commitment to that interest or activity must be genuine.

Faking an interest in something, just for the sake of being a member of that group, will not withstand time and the other demands a group can impose on its members. Unfortunately, too many teenagers fake enthusiasm to ensure their being included in the group.

A rule of thumb would be this: If the teenager would hold this interest, with or without the connection to the members of the group, then the interest is genuine. If teenagers invest positive energy in some project or interest that is meaningful to them, then others in the group will undoubtedly respond to this energy. This will occur, not because the teenager asks for it, but because it will naturally result from contagious enthusiasm.

Activity Can Create Positive Change

When teenagers put their interests to work, they can expand their group alliances through activity. For example, 4-H students in rural communities mark their progress in their teen years and their organization by raising livestock and competing for blue ribbons. They ride horses together and learn about how to farm. Teenagers in athletics play their sports together, earn their letters, and learn the value of team efforts.

Another example of shared activity is illustrated by a group of teenagers from one of San Francisco's toughest neighborhoods. In July 1994, these teenagers participated in Midnight Shakespeare, modeled after the popular Midnight Basketball programs held around the country. It involved inner-city teenagers who had little prior knowledge or interest in Shakespeare. In addition to successfully performing Hamlet, the performers developed a camaraderie that organizers said was a highlight of the experience.

In the spring of 1994, a Las Vegas group called PAZ-Latino—Possibilities Above Zero in the Latin Communities—demonstrated how different groups can unite for a greater purpose. PAZ-Latino worked out a truce between the city's Latino gangs in preparation for the annual Cinco de Mayo celebration. Beyond the time of that truce, the local Explorers division of the Boy Scouts of America established recreational and career opportunities for disadvantaged teenagers and young adults. The Boy Scouts worked with volunteer instructors to teach the gang youths everything from painting and sculpting to basic carpentry. Organizers said that, by teaching practical vocational skills to these youths, the gang members would have new options to get involved with positive activities, and create rather than destroy. This program would encourage gang members to replace tagging gang graffiti on block walls on private property with painting magnificent murals in areas of high visibility.

Some teenagers do not have the option to join clubs or other organized activities. These teenagers go to work instead. They hold part-time jobs during high school. This employment often preempts traditional group involvement for them. Many working teenagers, however, take advantage of the work place to build lasting friendships. With their co-workers they might share after-work activities, recreational interests, or career goals. Working teenagers have their own ways to build lasting friendships, many of which that will grow with them into adulthood.

Although not able to participate in normal group activities, working teenagers enjoy other advantages as well. According to a 1989 study by the Educational Testing Service, students who work twenty or fewer hours weekly have better grades than students who do not work at all. They also have the potential after high school to earn as much as twenty-two percent more than classmates who did not work. This success results, at least in part, from the connection between teenagers working in their senior year, and their later transition into the work place.

Other Dimensions of Belonging

Group membership also involves the dimensions of time and space. Each of these contributing factors will influence the strength of participation in, and identification with, the group.

Time Together

Teenagers who enjoy their group membership will seek opportunities to spend time together. In the early stages, belonging to a group requires nurturing. One of the best ways to accomplish this involves sharing time with each other.

Friends are people who prefer to spend time together, especially in the teen years. They enjoy each other's company. This does not mean that being the member of a group requires a prescribed time commitment. Rather, people who belong to a group generally prefer shared time with their group friends. Shared time reinforces closeness and support—two of the driving forces for joining a group in the first place.

Sharing time also means that friends make themselves available for one other. They are there for each other when the need arises. I often call these friends my "2 AM friends." They are the people I can call, and who can call me, at 2 AM, and know that we will be available to each other for any reason or purpose.

Some adolescents, however, need more time alone than others. They prefer to avoid the crowding that contact with others might impose. This does not mean that they do not enjoy their friendships; they just prefer less group time.

> "I used to want people to hang out with, something to do, something to occupy time. Now I like to be alone, or at home. My friends are those with whom I enjoy the time we spend together. A close friend is someone who knows my heart, my feelings, and my personality . . . always."
>
> *Mallie, 18, Leadership*

Place and Space

Teenagers who want to get the most from their groups will make more than time for their friends. They will find places to share this time with them. When they are able to share time in the same place, doing the same things, teenagers have better opportunities to enhance their emotional connections.

> "Sharing interests with group members is an important consideration. If you have nothing in common, there might not be a reason for spending time with them."
>
> *LiAn, 16, Scholastic*

> "It's nice to relate with other people and share mutual thoughts, even opposing thoughts on certain subjects."
>
> *Alyssa, 15, Letterman*

> "My friends and I have what we call 'bum time' together when we just hang around someone's house and talk. We share secrets, braid hair, and take time out from our busy lives for each other."
>
> *Kristy, 17, Religious*

> "When I am by myself I don't feel as confident about myself as I do when I'm with my friends. My friends cheer me up and make me feel good about myself, and this helps us get along better with everyone."
>
> *Kassi, 14, Rural*

Of course, doing things together can serve a purpose. But it is also important for teenagers to budget time that does nothing more than provide fun. As I mentioned in chapter 1, teenagers need play time in the same way their parents find recreation critical to their own search for balanced lives.

Encounters

Brief but intense friendship-like relationships arise when teenagers find themselves in situations that separate them from their daily routines of school, activities, and friends. These *encounters* can occur when circumstances—event, time, and place—create "instant bonding" between teenagers who are experiencing the same situation, often somewhere other than home.

- Teenagers stranded at an airport in another city during a hurricane.
- Cross-town sports rivals who cheer each other on during a national athletic competition two time zones away.
- Adolescents who attend a regional theater group for a week in the summer.

Crises, or other threatening situations closer to home, can also throw teenagers together. These teenagers might not even know each other, or not know each other well, or even prefer to avoid association with each other. Yet, these encounters can create immediate bonding.

- A bomb threat that sends all classes outside the school building.
- The suicide of a high school sophomore that links an entire student body.
- A mini-van, loaded with ski club members, that skids off an icy road on the way home from a day trip.

Although encounters can produce intense involvements and instant relationships based on a "common experience," they generally have short life spans.

Quick Points

- When teenagers move into the group-friendship stage of their lives, they often move into a process of "merging" with their friends.
- During the merger process, teenagers discover what they share in common with their group friends.
- Teenage groups adopt distinctive symbols to describe who they are and why they are different from others. Obvious demonstrations of membership can include clothing, symbols, and tastes in music.
- Language also helps identify group membership, especially in gangs.
- Language means more than words. It includes various demonstrations of the "words" of friendship.
- When teenagers share the same interests—like the same things—they take a giant step toward building friendship in their group.
- Activity in the group can create positive change.
- Some teenagers—often those who work part-time—do not have the option to join clubs or organized activities. Yet, they experience benefits from the employment experience.
- Group membership also involves the dimensions of time and space.
- Teenagers in groups usually seek opportunities to spend time together.
- Sharing time also means that friends make themselves available to one another in times of need.
- Some people need more time alone than others.
- Teenagers who want to get the most from their groups also make an effort to find places to share time.
- Sometimes, teenagers will form groups when they otherwise would not. These *encounters,* often founded on unexpected circumstances, usually result in intense friendships that are brief.

6
Seeking Significance, Plotting Purpose

From the very first day of school, Randy experienced a nagging feeling every time he spotted his counselor, even at a distance. "By the time you enter your senior year," his counselor had repeatedly told him, "teenagers should know what they want to do with their lives." This recurring message pervaded his thoughts, as he turned over in his bed to get up every morning. As a younger boy, breakfast was a time when he focused his attention on the calendar positioned prominently on the refrigerator. He would delight in the vision of the red marks that indicated school vacations, and eagerly count the days until they would arrive. Now he avoided counting days. This only marked the nearness of change in his life. Fortunately, Randy had his buddies. Basketball bonded them throughout high school, and now that the season had passed, they continued to spend time together at the video arcade, movies, and parties. He always felt better when he thought about them. Randy realized that he and his group would hang in there for each other, whenever they needed it. Especially now.

Whenever parents talk with their teenagers, one of the universal statements they often assert goes something like this: "Kids have never had it so good. When I was your age. . . ." Unfortunately, from all directions, experts challenge the presumption that teenagers have it easy or soft. In fact, today's teenagers are experiencing elevated levels of stress, fear, disappointment, and more. Many influences contribute to these physical, social, and psychological phenomena, which often result from unrealistic expectations of themselves and others: Complex family situations, multimedia presence, scholastic pressures, societal expectations, too-negative or too-positive stereotypes, and so on.

Stress

Considering these issues, teenagers have learned to turn to their groups for some of their greatest reassurances. They seek out their friends to paint positive survive-and-surpass messages on their own life portraits. To transcend their adolescent years—with all of the complexities that ensue—teenagers recognize they need to resolve the stress in their lives.

Stress and Identity

Most teenagers at one time or another probably find themselves saying: "How much of this am I supposed to take?" "What should I do?" "I don't know if I can do this alone." In their deepest moments of stress, many teenagers will even question their own identities, "Who am I, anyway, Super-Achiever?"

To a reasonable extent, teenagers can become stronger by experiencing a certain amount of push-pull on their bodies, challenges to their minds, and temporary upheavals in their emotions. These less-than-stable states enlist teenagers in the process of questioning status quo and the comfort it can provide. They learn to seek answers or create their own solutions: problem-solving at its best. They learn that taking risks can, and often does, produce positive results.

Because teenagers strive to survive the perceived limbo of their seven-year adolescent stage, they generally turn to many other people before, if ever, turning to their parents. In these years of personal revolt, teenagers need to pull away from the identities their parents have given them.

Stress in adolescents creates other distinctive challenges because, at the same time teens are suffering from stressful situations, they are still developing. Their minds and their bodies are growing. Unfortunately, their perspectives and their reactions to stress probably remain stuck in their past. Of course, this dilemma creates additional stress and confusion.

Teens search for support, without the imposition of additional stress and imposed standards for performance. Thus, the group—friends—offers substantial assistance in times of stress. They understand; they are going through the same experience.

Although teenagers rely on their groups for help in times of stress, they need to learn to rely on themselves more than anyone else. Adolescents need to realize many of the situations that produce psychological stress involve some level of conflict between the teenager and society itself. As long as teenagers continue to satisfy the social demand, at the cost of their own personal identities, or vice versa, they will continue to feel the strain of stress.

So, adolescents need to create a balance that will help reduce stress, starting with feeling good about themselves and their identities. This healthy self-esteem can empower teenagers to attain perspective, which has great power in easing stressful situations for them.

Reducing Stress with Coping Skills

Stress is a response to a perceived demand for action. Few people succeed in escaping stress, whether negative or positive. So, when teenagers need to do something and cannot, they tend to experience physical, emotional, and psychological stress. However, teenagers, with the help and support of their parents, can learn how to cope with stress in positive ways. They can:

- *Seize control in small ways.* Teenagers should take the opportunity to put order into their lives where they can.
- *Practice positive thinking.* Teenagers should pat them-

selves on the back as often as possible, and put positive thoughts to work.

- *Stop anguishing.* When teenagers continue to fret over all of those "what if" situations in their lives, they create negative situations for their thinking and their potential. They need to stop beating themselves up for what is past and done, and replace this thinking with problem-solving alternatives and options for present and future actions.
- *Set priorities.* Teenagers often allow themselves to be overwhelmed by surrendering to others' expectations, or imposing extraordinary demands on themselves. They need to determine what is realistic and important to them, and not let every outside force dictate their choices.
- *Create opportunities for privacy.* Teenagers need to schedule time and place for private time so that they can think through their situations and the demands on their lives. Private time empowers them to avoid cluttered intrusions from the outside.
- *Be good to themselves.* Teenagers need to learn how to develop perspective, giving themselves a break from stress. Physical and emotional breaks are important, with opportunities arising in physical exercise and balanced diet.
- *Respond to "preferences."* Other than life's basic needs for food, water, clothing, and shelter, everything else is a preference. Teenagers will experience self-satisfaction when they make decisions based on their own preferences, rather than those imposed upon them by others. This does not mean that teenagers are exempt from following the rules. It does mean that they should practice being accountable to themselves first.
- *Keep life simple.* Teenagers should learn how to take a distant look at what pressures them so that they can see the "bigger picture." This will help them add perspective to their thoughts and activities.
- *Maintain healthy bodies.* This includes a personal workout program and a reasonable diet. Also, teens need adequate sleep when facing stressful situations.
- *Do one thing at a time.* Teenagers can avoid overloading

themselves by understanding what they need to do, and in what order. By avoiding overload, teenagers are much better equipped to handle their tasks and responsibilities.

When all else fails, teenagers can put *humor* to work. Laughter helps increase blood circulation and feeds oxygen to the brain. It also increases endorphins—those little physiological bits of magic that help enhance the body's immune system, reduce pain, and improve mental skills. Teenagers can create opportunities for laughter through their interactions with each other—jokes, stories, and shared experiences. They can seek humor through reading books, magazines, the newspaper, cartoon books, and so on. The media also provide vast opportunities for laughter in movies, television, radio, video, CD, and more.

Choices: Victim or Master

Teenagers should remember that whatever happens in their lives is not the issue; how they react to situations is. *Self-awareness* can enhance how teenagers handle their stress.

Regularly, I work with residents of several youth institutions. In my various communications classes sit teenagers with diverse concerns and problems. As they enter the room, they inevitably "size me up," wonder just what the program is all about, and . . . ponder why I think I can help them.

The first message I share is gentle, but firm. I tell the teenagers that they have the ability and opportunity to control the way they respond to their situations and their environments. They can master the stress of institutional restraint in their lives.

"You are not victims," I tell them. "You have the ability to control how you respond to whatever happens to you in your life." They never fail to ask me how I know, or think I could understand, what they are going through.

I explain to them that many of us are "prisoners" in our own ways. Many of us suffer from "addictions" that can hurt us: Drugs, alcohol, gambling, dangerous risk-taking, power. . . .

Often, we let the stress of our lives overpower us, and succumb to our addictions.

They look at me again, and wonder what my addiction is. I tell them: "I am a recovering anorexic." I first acquired the eating disorder during my second year of law school in 1978. To feel "in control" of the grinding process of legal education, I took control of my eating and my exercise. Unfortunately, I suffered a neurological injury because of my starvation, and had to quit law school five weeks before the end of my third year. For every day since then, I have dealt with the effects of its presence in my life. Every time I eat just a little too much, I fight the near-automatic impulse to purge. Stress, and a need to control my life, changed my life.

My group—my friends—who then, as now, helped me find within myself the ability to master my own life, one day at a time. So far, so good. And so I tell the teenagers:

> Each day, find one way to create change—positive change—so that when you eventually find your way to the other side, you will not be the same person you were coming in. This changed person will be the person who is willing and able to turn negative behavior into positive thoughts and actions. It's all up to you. Your group can offer support and encouragement, and that is crucial in the process. But, nobody else can rid you of the stress of change, just you. And there's no better time to start than right now.

Other teenagers can learn a message from these dialogues. Adolescents should accept responsibility for their own thoughts and actions. They cannot dwell on the negatives from their past that might try to pull them down. They must learn lessons—tough lessons—from what is past, and move forward. They must reverse the idea that they might be victims, and turn this attitude into a positive one. Teenagers have the ability to reduce the stress in their lives by denying a victim-identity, and accepting the positive identity as masters of their lives.

Fear

So far this chapter has focused on the impact of stress in the lives of teenagers. Closely related to stress is fear. Like stress, fear does not have to provoke negative responses. Both factors—stress and fear—can stimulate positive activity and create beneficial results. Weighing word choices and attitudes, a teenager's first assertive choice in dealing with fear would involve renaming that fear. "Excitement." Then, they can turn fear's depleting potential into positive energy. To understand this better, let's look at the basics of fear.

From the Beginning

Most teenagers treat fear as a negative force. This can happen because parents often use fear to keep their young children safe from harm. Because parents cannot always be available to protect their children, fear serves as their proxy. "Fear *everything,* just in case *something* could hurt you." Crossing streets, meeting strangers, eating Halloween candy. . . .

As children grow into adolescents, they learn to differentiate between harmful influences and safe ones. They demonstrate this especially well when they decide to do what they might fear. By *doing* what they fear, teenagers can turn fear into energy. They learn to distinguish between activities that are truly dangerous and those that are merely fresh and untried.

Worrying has played an integral part—a learned part—in human behavior since the beginning of time, according to Terry Gingras, a clinical psychologist at the Behavioral Medicine Institute. "Worry doesn't really help you with your problems. It can wear you out. You need to think instead about problem-solving." Teenagers need to find ways to convert their fears into energy, to expand these rushed tensions into physical energy.

For example, instead of letting their bodies tense up over an exam, teenagers can work out for an hour as a study break the night before the test. Or, when they feel stressed about a problem with their parents, teens can take a brisk three-mile walk. Or, they can put that nervous energy into a karate session.

In addition to the fears of not being accepted (See chapter 4 on "belonging"), teenagers experience substantial fears of failure, making mistakes, and . . . success.

Fear of Failure

Few, if any of us, like to fail. Especially teenagers who are working each day to stabilize their identities. They do not want to fail tests, nor lose at sporting competition, nor be dumped by their boyfriends and girlfriends. What most teenagers do not realize, probably because they have not had a lot of experience at it yet, is that failure serves as a prerequisite for success. In starting the journey toward acceptance of failure as a natural learning step, one message prevails: We do not have control over all beginnings, middles, and conclusions. We do, however, have the ultimate control over how we perceive and respond to this process. Failure means different things to teenagers:

" . . . Losing to a lesser opponent."

Alyssa, 15, Letterman

" . . . Snitching on each other."

Dedric, 16, Gang

" . . . When you have done nothing, and don't even try to do anything."

Kassi, 14, Rural

" . . . Not getting along, excluding others, being judgmental toward each other."

Tera, 16, Religious

" . . . Not being able to go after what we want."

Charla, 15, SADD

" . . . Getting strung out on drugs."

Jason, 17, Gang

" . . . Giving excuses to make up for wrongs."

Michael, 16, Leadership

" . . . Making my parents ashamed of me in any way."

Mayte, 19, Cultural

" . . . When a homeboy gets shot."

Jeremy, 17, Gang

Teenagers have viable options to help them deal with failure, and turn negatives into positives. They can:

- *Accept that no one is perfect.* Not being perfect is actually an asset. Knowing this, teenagers should remember that the only way to avoid failure is to do nothing. Where does doing nothing get them? Nowhere!
- *Avoid blaming others.* By taking responsibility, teenagers can understand their own potential, and their own limitations. They need to admit their errors and seek reasonable solutions to their problems.
- *Define and apply focus.* Teenagers should determine what they want to accomplish, and keep their attention on this goal until they achieve it—even if they do not reach the planned or expected end. The journey itself will help them get closer to accomplishing the next goal.
- *Do their homework.* Teenagers learn the importance of doing their school work. When they are thorough, they enjoy the rewards of a job well done. The same principle applies to everything else they might consider important, from sports to social events to group commitments.
- *Be willing to break away from their safety zones.* Teenagers who are willing to "take risks" create opportunities to enjoy success in new ways.
- *Set sights on success.* When teenagers believe in their abilities to succeed, they have a much greater chance to experience success.

- *Let failure propel them forward.* Life is full of failures. Rather than letting one failure lead to the next, teenagers should let one failure provide the foundation for the next success.

Group support can enhance these suggestions for dealing with failure. Teenagers who are especially vulnerable to the idea of failure should strive to surround themselves with a group of friends that reinforces the idea of success: friends who trust and believe in teenagers and their efforts to succeed. Ironically, teens who struggle with failure often have the most difficulty in finding friends who focus on success. By relating to more successful teenagers, however, they will have a better chance to find the stimulation to succeed.

Fear of Making Mistakes

Mistakes are related to stress and fear, because they link two important elements in the chain of learning. They connect the willingness to try with the acceptance of unplanned results. Mistakes do not necessarily translate into failure, contrary to what most people perceive. Instead of being ends in themselves, mistakes show teenagers that what they are doing needs improving. Mistakes teach teenagers what *not* to do. Without mistakes, how would teenagers know what "next step" might be the best step?

Ordinarily, the fear of making mistakes results from *expectations,* often expectations for the unreachable accomplishment: perfection. Even when the level of desire does top at perfection, teenagers can hurl self-defeat on themselves by expecting themselves to:

- Do things perfectly.
- Accomplish more in a day.
- Do everything that other people expect them to do.
- Prove themselves to everyone else.
- Find satisfaction in what they do, because they are supposed to.
- Strive for "it all" because society says so.

- Put off fun until all of the serious stuff is done.
- Weigh their own value by how other people accept them.
- Be everything to everybody.

For some unknown reason, most people consider mistakes as actions that reflect personal unworthiness. That mistakes measure weaknesses and failures. Yet, no one is perfect. In fact, imperfection prompts mistakes. Mistakes prompt better performance. Better performance prompts ultimate success. *Voila*. The process, from start to finish.

Fear of Success

Fearing ultimate success prompts many teenagers not to try at all. Yes, the fear of accomplishing something perceived by others as positive often spooks teenagers as much as the fear of failure and the fear of making mistakes. Why?

Many teenagers think that success is a "rationed reward"—only so much to go around. If they get their share of success, then somebody else, from somewhere else, will take something very important away from them in retribution of the earlier success. An excellent grade on one exam will naturally translate into a lower grade somewhere later in the semester. A winning score in a basketball game will be evened out with fouling out later in the season. A date with the most popular person in the class will require dates with nerds for the rest of the year. That's just the way it works, right?

The fear of success reflects, in part, a response to the pressures that surround teenagers today. From every direction—home, school, the media, high technology, and even friends—teenagers are reminded that "winning is everything." Pressure to succeed naturally follows this philosophy.

Just as with failure, however, teenagers have their own ways to define success:

> " . . . Doing well in games, achieving high goals, a big 'W' (win) in the stats."

> *Alyssa, 15, Letterman*

" . . . Knowing that we've done our best, and always will."

Kassi, 14, Rural

" . . . Accomplishing our goals."

Tera, 16, Religious

" . . . Appearing successful and responsible. . . . Out-scoring and out-performing others."

Karim, 17, Leadership

" . . . Becoming an OG (Original Gangster), and making it without snitching, being crippled, or dying."

Jason, 17, Gang

" . . . Completing an activity."

Charla, 15, SADD

" . . . Being able to say I gave it my all."

Michael, 16, Leadership

" . . . Getting someone back if they shoot a homeboy."

Jeremy, 17, Gang

" . . . Being happy, never forgetting where I came from, and making my parents proud."

Mayte, 19, Cultural

" . . . Moving in the direction of achieving a personal goal."

Mallie, 18, Leadership

" . . . Hanging together at all times."

Dedric, 16, Gang

Definitions for success are as individual as fingerprints. Within the loose parameters of society, teenagers must define and apply the principles of success that work for them. Why should we give them so much "room" to explore? Because teenagers will also be responsible for measuring and altering their own progress on the personal success continuum. Rather than driving for the victory, teenagers need to be reassured that their efforts, and their willingness to make mistakes, comprise the most important steps toward success they can take. After all, no teenager can be the best at everything. However, without making the effort (and the mistakes), how will teenagers learn which choices are the best choices? This goes for scholastics, sports, socializing, family interactions, group activities, and more.

The Power of Positive Thinking, Then . . . Doing

Thinking positive thoughts about ability and potential can open the door for teenagers. This sounds like something from one of those self-help books that most teenagers would quickly pass in a book store—on their way to something more contemporary and personally enlightening. Often, teenagers allow themselves to be dominated by thoughts inspired by flash, velocity, and promise. When they do this, however, teenagers should stop long enough to ponder one reality: Thinking alone won't hack it. Thoughts without actions exist in a vacuum, with their life and energy sucked from them within nanoseconds of their mental creation. Teenagers do not want to believe that their thoughts have no value. If they accept this valueless-ness, how will it affect their desires or inclinations to attempt anything? To make the effort? To risk mistakes? To expose themselves to failure? To invite success?

Leadership Las Vegas Youth teaches a lofty philosophy, but not so lofty that it is either unreasonable or unreachable.

"Vision without action is merely a dream. Action without vision just passes the time. Vision with action can change the world."

The Value of Affirmation

By making firm, solid, and specific their important thoughts, teenagers can move forward, step by step, to turn their thoughts into realities. To accomplish this, teens can use the process of *affirmation*. It begins with an "assignment": Teenagers should write down their aspirations. They should then repeat over and over again—mentally and orally—what is important to them and what they want to accomplish. Each affirmation or exercise in *self talk* should start with "I" and be followed by a verb in the present tense, such as "I am" or "I want" or "I do." I *am* an honor-roll student. I *want* to go to Yale when I graduate from high school. I *do* provide the best service of any employee at the video store.

This "present voice" helps teenagers accept their thoughts as authentic. They can solidify their ideas, making them more real with each restated effort. Ideally, of course, teenagers will repeat positive affirmations to accomplish successes that benefit themselves and others.

Group membership can provide distinctive advantages and disadvantages to teenagers who practice self talk. Groups can help individual members determine the directions they want to travel, in the short-run and long-term. Members can help each other recognize the reality of their expectations, and help themselves feel good about their efforts.

However, groups can work in the opposite way to discourage their members by making fun of their commitments to thinking, affirming, and creating their own destinies. Minimally, members can experience "confusion" when they do not enjoy group support.

> "Right now I am confused about who I am, but feel my education is very important. However, when I see my friends from the neighborhood, they say I am 'selling out' or that I am embarrassed about them. But, I am not. The people from the university tell me I need to grow up and get out of my old habits. So, my loyalties are messed up."
> *Mayte, 19, Cultural*

When the group has provided a strong support system for the teen member, they will probably help each other—affirming each other and their individual thoughts, expectations, and realities.

> "What I expect from myself and others in the group is a big consideration when I choose friends. I expect all of us to be supportive of each other in the group."
>
> *LiAn, 16, Scholastic*

> "I expect everyone, including myself, to have respect for themselves and everyone else, not just in the group. They need to be themselves and not try to be 'cool.' "
>
> *Natalie, 17, Choir*

Putting Off . . .

When teenagers face the fear of failure, the fear of making a mistake, or the fear of success, they often procrastinate in their actions. They put off as much as they possibly can. This act of avoiding actions usually results in postponement, not permanent escape. The act of avoidance, however, does produce stress that enhances the challenge. So let's consider some ways that teenagers, with the consistent support of their parents, can help themselves by forgoing detours. They can:

- *Identify the fear.* Often the fear itself is not rational. It does not even make sense when the teenager thinks it through or talks about it.
- *Analyze the task or idea being avoided.* Teenagers should break down the task, project, or idea they are avoiding into manageable "chunks" of thought or activity. This helps them turn what once seemed overwhelming into something manageable.
- *Weigh the consequences.* Teenagers should weigh alternatives, considering the best and the worst of outcomes. Then, they should consider what impact they can have on either.
- *Take the first step.* It would be easy to limit themselves to the thought stages of ideas and tasks. However, to get closer to success, teenagers must take the first step.

- *Dump the excuses*. Teenagers should rid themselves of the many great excuses that might prevent them from beginning, working through, and completing the formation of their ideas, and the execution of their actions.

Turning to the Group

To overcome the fears of failure, making mistakes, and achieving success, teenagers do not need to balance pain with success to satisfy some higher order. However, thinking this thought of gain-then-pain can make it so.

Groups can assert a powerful influence over their members in relieving stress and the various fears I have discussed in this chapter. The group, with its ability to provide united support and assurance, can help its members survive and surpass these influences. However, just as with stress, each individual group member must look inside to let "self" give the ultimate directions.

Quick Points

- Today's teenagers are experiencing elevated levels of stress, fear, and disappointment.
- Teenagers turn to their groups for answers and reassurances during times of stress.
- At one time or another, most teenagers question their capabilities and identities.
- A reasonable amount of stress can provide positive opportunities for teenagers.
- Teenagers need to learn to rely on themselves in stressful times.
- Few teenagers succeed in escaping stress, even when it is positive.
- Stress is a response to a perceived demand for action. Several ways teens can cope with stress include:
  - ↤ Seizing control in small ways.
  - ↤ Practicing positive thinking.
  - ↤ Stopping distress.

- Setting priorities.
- Creating opportunities for privacy.
- Being good to themselves.
- Responding to "preferences."
- Keeping life simple.
- Maintaining healthy bodies.
- Doing one thing at a time.

- Teenagers can also handle stress by putting humor to work.
- Self-awareness will help teenagers work through their stress.
- Teenagers have choices of whether to consider themselves victims of their stress or masters of their direction.
- Most teenagers allow fear to paralyze them. They treat it as a negative force.
- The fear of failure prompts many teenagers to avoid action. Yet, failure serves as the prerequisite to many of the most important successes.
- To excel in efforts to deal with failure, teenagers should:
  - Realize that no one is perfect.
  - Accept responsibility.
  - Define and apply focus.
  - Do their homework.
  - Be willing to break away from safety zones.
  - Set sights on success.
  - Let failure propel them forward.

- Mistakes show teenagers that what they are doing needs improvement.
- Ordinarily, the fear of making mistakes results from expectations.
- Fearing ultimate success can prompt teenagers not to try at all.
- Teenagers have difficulty in meeting the standards set by the "winning is everything" pressure imposed upon them.
- Thinking positive thoughts about ability and potential can open doors for teenagers.

- *Affirmations* or positive *self talk* can reinforce the transition between mere thought and definitive action. Self talk works best when teenagers think and speak in the first person— *I*—and a present tense word—*am . . . do . . . want. . . .*
- Group membership can provide distinctive advantages and disadvantages for teenagers who use affirmations.
- Teenagers who experience stress and fears often procrastinate to avoid their thoughts and actions.
- Groups can assert powerful influence over their members, and the ways they handle stress and fears. Groups can help members by offering reassurance and support.

7
Putting Power to Work

Tracy and Patrick had grown up in the same neighborhood. They had gone to each other's birthdays, attended the same schools, and hung out with the same crowd. They considered their friendship sacred and knew that "more than anything in the world" they would always be close. In school, with their friends, around their families, they were secure with the comfort and confidence that surrounded them. . . . until Tracy started to wonder why other people—even her friends—always told her what to do. Her parents would tell her: "Pick up your clothes." Her teachers imposed on her the repeated message: "Finish your assignment or you will have to stay after school." Her friends controlled her with: "You can only come to the movie with us if you pay." Even Patrick crowded her life with mandates and commands. For the first time she could remember, Tracy wondered just how much control she had over her life, anyway!

The push and pull of the adolescent years often peaks with a *struggle for power*—a time when teenagers presume that they have no dominion over their own lives. They believe that all decisions—important and not—come from a "higher power": parents, teachers, even peers. Sometimes, this is true. But, often it results from forfeiture, the giving-up of responsible decision making.

Searching for Power:
The Role of the Parent

As teenagers progress through their adolescence, one of the major adjustments they experience revolves around *authority*. Their need to understand the impact of authority involves the role that parents and other adults play in their lives. Equally important for teens: Their peer group and, eventually, themselves.

Control: From the Parents' Perspective

Although most teenagers demonstrate responsibility in making decisions for themselves, they sometimes lack the consistent ability to make long-term decisions. They ponder the choices and know that they can turn to their parents or their friends. The group provides a sanctuary, where teens can soften the impact of parental wrath and authoritarianism.

The vast majority of teens still need to go home at some point, and respond to their parents and their parents' authority. Sometimes it takes a while, but teens generally recognize that their parents have something of value to say. They also accept—at least momentarily—their parents' assertion of authority. Knowing this, parents should respect their teenagers' abilities to understand the parameters of parental authority.

Parents also should help their teens learn how to adapt their own thinking and values to daily living. This will help teenagers learn how to mature into adult decision-makers, complete with the ability to live by their own decisions. HOBY participants recognized the importance of personal responsibility. Fifty-nine percent of them believed that they already had the primary responsibility for their own thoughts and behaviors.

As teenagers get older, they tend to have a better understanding of what parents and other people with authority expect of them. They learn how to adapt their own behaviors with what is socially and legally acceptable. Yet, they also learn how to carve out their identities and independence. This comprises an important aspect of their own personal evolution.

Parental Styles Influence Teenagers

The style of parenting determines the kind of relationship parents have with their children, especially when it comes to defining and delineating authority. Teenagers, in turn, learn these styles and apply them to their own behavior within their groups. After all, most of what they initially learn, they learn at home.

According to Don Fleming, author of *How to Stop the Battle with Your Teenager* (Fireside, 1989), *overcritical* parents believe that they can teach their teenagers about life by telling them everything they are doing wrong. Unfortunately, this usually results in the teenager's hatred of the parent's voice and opinions. Also, parents who constantly tell their teenagers how incompetent they are, impose feelings of helplessness and inability on their teens. What impact does this have on teens and their friends? Overcritical offspring sometimes become overcritical friends. They might tend to look for what is wrong with their friends, not what is right.

Other parenting styles can wreak comparable havoc in teenagers' lives. Combative parents lose both verbal control and authority. Frequently, these parents do not know their teenagers, yet they think that they are teaching their teenagers about life and values. Of course, combative parents also believe that their teenagers should accept these opinions without question, without argument. But arguments inevitably ensue. How do teens translate their parents' behavior into their relationships with their group? They often create and perpetuate arguments within their groups, which puts additional and unnecessary stress into the mix.

Some parents want to be *friendly*. These parents tend to be overly tolerant, demonstrating little or no authority. They accept most of their teenager's behavior and want to add a "pal" element to the fun times and conversations. Unfortunately, by relinquishing their authority, these parents also avoid setting necessary limits and boundaries. Their teenagers discover these restrictions for themselves. Teenagers still need adults in their lives, so this might prompt them to look outside the home for adult guidance. How does this affect their friendships? They might lean exclusively on their group to help them with important decisions and directions.

Absent parents reflect the times. They do not share as much time or activity with their teenagers. By circumstance or choice, these parents commit little time to parenting, yet hope that their teenagers will be mature enough to "figure it out for themselves." What results? Teenagers who tend to resent rules, reject structure, and have difficulty in the growing-up process. More and more teens live in homes where parents appear—and disappear—with regularity. So, what part does the group play? These teens often reach out to their groups to fill the parental void. They know that they can seek out their friends to fill the lost time, the lost activity, the lost input.

Parents who assert too much control—*authoritarian* parents—send a clear message to their teenagers: "I'm the boss, so what I say goes." Many parents rely on this style because they have had problems with their teenagers, and feel this is their only parenting choice. However, over-controlling parents tend to overlook their teenager's struggles for independence and opportunities to express other feelings. This form of parenting can damage the teenager and the relationship between parent and child. Again, the group might fill the void as a "family that cares" for the teen; and . . . a teen who cares for the "family."

Some parents assert their authority over their teenagers by becoming *outrageous*. They respond to behavior that they do not like by throwing temper tantrums or blowing their cool. Their teenagers get the brunt of these reactions. By overreacting, these parents lose their contact with their teenagers. Teens learn to ignore or tune out their own parents' words and behavior. We see evidence of this in some of the antisocial behavior in our country. Teenagers often mimic their parents' hostile behaviors, especially when they see so much of it at home. In anger and frustration, these teenagers often turn to groups that demonstrate similar behaviors and forms of control over others.

Then there are the parents who recognize and appreciate the value of *responsible* parenting. They want to assert themselves as the adults—the parents—in their families. They set proper limits and monitor their teenagers. As their teenagers mature, these parents respect their children's evolution and abilities to make decisions for themselves. They trust their children to the degree their teenagers demonstrate respect and responsibility. They know when to talk, and when to listen. Responsible parents communicate openly with their children, and invite their teenagers to be assertive and responsible. *Consistency* serves as a watchword for these parents. Teens from these families have the opportunity to develop healthy friendships and enhance their groups.

The parenting style adults adopt will directly impact the teenager. It will also affect the teenager's group—the friends who not only offer support through the growing-up years, but also experience parenting styles in their own homes. These parent-choices will influence teenagers in the ways they react to conflict, praise, punishment, reward, goal-setting, and more. And these choices will affect the other people in their lives, particularly their friends.

Punishment: An Unwelcome Response

When parents deal with their teenagers' negative behaviors, they have options. They can ignore negative behavior and hope that it will go away. Or, they can connect with a particular parenting style explained in the previous section.

Or, as happens most often, parents can punish their teenagers for negative behavior. By punishing their children, parents deprive these teenagers of certain activities or privileges for a specified period of time. "No parties for the rest of your life!" might ring through the house when parents vocalize their immediate reactions for unexpected or disappointing behavior. Even teen groups issue similar forms of punishment. Often, of course, these reprimands are issued in anger and frustration. Time has a way of tempering permanent or extreme punishments.

"In my group, punishment might translate into academic probation, being pushed to do better in your classes, or the loss of privilege in sports and other outside activities."

Jasmine, 16, Scholastic

"It's not for my group to punish me. However, they might ignore me."

Amber, 14, Social

"My friends might say, 'Good luck next time'."

Thomas, 16, Rural

"Sometimes, my group gives me the silent treatment, depending on the severity of my action. If worse, they might use harsh words, or even fight with me."

Jennifer, 16, Social

" . . . Being publicly known for not carrying out a task."

Neil, 17, Leadership

Often, parents rely on punishment as a primary source of "teaching lessons" to their teenagers for negative behavior. If so, they should remember to "connect" the punishment with the behavior they are punishing. When parents use such expressions as: "You are being punished for your own good," teenagers struggle to understand what negative behavior prompted this response. Adolescents need to see connections between the behavior and the punishment. For example, a teenager who takes a sibling's favorite sweater without asking might be punished by having to wash her sister's clothes for a month. By making this connection between the ill-received activity and the punishment, the teenager learns that consequences follow prohibited behaviors.

Better still, parents should look for alternatives to punishment. One option is *constructive review,* which forty-one percent of HOBY survey participants said they "most readily receive" from their parents. For example, parents can sit down with their teenager on report card day. They can talk about the grades and discuss possible ways for the teenager to pull up less-than-satisfactory grades. Parents should let their teenagers offer most of the suggestions, because they will have to deliver on the solutions for improvement.

Parents can also give teenagers opportunities for "taking responsibility" for their actions and offering their own *corrective action*. For example, when a teenager brings the car home dirty, parents should acknowledge that the car returned in a different state of cleanliness than it left the home. Then, the parents can ask the teenager how he or she plans to correct this. Let the teenager suggest the alternative, maybe by offering to wash the car on Saturday. This gives the teenager a chance to make amends, feel good about finding solutions, and acting upon them.

Other alternatives to punishment involve various forms of discipline. Parents can:

- Express strong disapproval through candid communication.
- State their expectations in advance of—and following— the behavior.
- Give the teenager choices for behavior.
- Take action, but not punitive action.
- Allow the teenager to experience the consequences of the negative behavior.

When parents consider these alternatives they can make tremendous strides. Discipline provides education. It helps parents direct their teenagers and lay the foundation for their teens to develop internal self-control, self-direction, and efficiency.

Praise and Reward: A Sound Alternative

So much of the time, parents focus their attention on what

teenagers are failing to do, what rules they are breaking, and how they are not meeting society's standards of performance. What a shame. This means that they ignore a vast, vast majority of today's teenagers—those adolescents who do live by the rules, take responsibility for their actions, and make positive contributions to themselves and others.

Just knowing that these contributors are overlooked and forsaken by society, parents will take a first step toward change. *Praise* works as a viable alternative. This gives parents ways to reconsider their relationship options. Praise empowers parents to *affirm* teenagers' behavior when it produces positive results. Of course, praise needs to be appropriate to the action and the teen's level of ability and accomplishment. Parents need to remember, too, that in all situations—whatever the level of success or failure—their teenagers will look to them as an ongoing resource for love, appreciation, and acceptance.

Praise, like criticism, can be destructive, especially when parents use absolute language, such as "always" and "never." These words place too much pressure on teens. They create too much anxiety, and make future behavior too difficult to handle.

Also, praise should describe the act or behavior. It should not include descriptions of personality or character. By praising personality traits, parents again place an excessive burden on their teens. "You always perform your best in school" can be too much to handle for a teenager who might bring home a B on his next report card.

Praise consists of two parts: What parents say to their teenagers, and what those teens, in turn, say to themselves. Parents' words should state what they *like* and *appreciate* about the teen's efforts, assistance, work, accomplishments. The teenager will then draw *conclusions* and internalize them. So, when parents describe events and feelings realistically and appreciatively, their teenagers are likely to conclude that they are positive and productive.

In praising their teens for action, parents need to be careful not to use the praise as a putdown for a past action that did not succeed. They should focus on the present strength and accomplishment.

Teenagers need praise that helps them accept their accomplishments because of their successful efforts, not merely because they met parental expectations. Parents need to augment their usual "I'm so proud of you for . . . " statements. When they enhance these messages with "You should feel very proud of yourself for. . . ," parents empower their teenagers to feel pride in themselves for their own actions. This distinction encourages teenagers to do well, not just to perform primarily to please someone else.

As the predominant authority figures in their teenager's life, parents have a responsibility to measure their teen's successes. They should accept their teen's mistakes as an important stage of learning. They also need to encourage their teens to apply these mistake-lessons to the eventual successes they will experience.

In addition, parents must realize that praise can create anxieties in their teens, by "setting them up" for their next performance at the same task. "You scored more points than ever. Job well done." Most teenagers will appreciate this support from their parents. Others, however, might be more sensitive and interpret it as: "Wow, what happens if I don't do that well the next time?"

How does the use of praise influence teenagers in their group settings? When teenagers feel good about themselves, they will generally transfer this high self-esteem to their relationships with others. Often, they will excel as performers within the group, because they do not feel threatened by their own abilities or the outcomes of their efforts.

"Membership in my group means recognition and the understanding that you get when you do something extra for yourself and others."

LiAn, 16, Scholastic

"To be a member of a group is important, because it is hard to stand alone. There is strength in numbers."

Kristy, 17, Religious

"For me, being in my group gives me a sense of accomplishment, getting somewhere, being somewhere, being someone, having something someone else wants."

Lisa, 16, Leadership

Authority among Teens

Many parents consider their teenager's group behavior as barbaric and uncontrolled, secretive, isolationist, and more. Whew. Where do teenagers go from there?

Testing Authority

Teenagers value their group behavior as one of the most enjoyable features of their teen years. Despite the perspective of many parents, group behavior allows the teen members to establish lifelong friendships. Being a member of the group also allows a teenager to "test authority." This might involve some negative behavior, sometimes even illegal behavior. This testing process can bring out the worst in teenagers.

- Staying out two hours past curfew, and doing it again even when their parents threaten restriction.
- Taking drugs, even though their parents and legal authorities ban it.
- Dating someone who is a 'bad influence' on them, and flaunting this at their parents.
- Skipping classes and getting caught, then doing it again a week later.
- Stealing books from a class reference section, and bragging about it to their friends.

Testing authority, however, can also bring out the best, even if it challenges parental authority.

- Going out of town with friends, against their parents' wishes, to participate in a music contest, and taking first-place honors in the competition.

- Failing to arrive home for dinner because they want to spend an extra hour in the library.
- Staying at a friend's house an hour past curfew to clean up the mess from a party.

Most of the time challenging authority gives teenagers the opportunity to "stretch" themselves and test their emerging identities and independence. By challenging imposed limits, adolescents learn how far they can go and still hold themselves accountable. The group offers teens an alternative refuge when their testing runs awry . . . even when their limit-challenging produces positive results. Most group behavior extends only to the extent of loudness, exhibitionism, and other public "nonsense." Why? Even in the group, usually one or two members will act as the authority figures for that group. They will exert the "parental" oversight for the group's activities and keep it in check.

Peer Conflicts

Even when the members of a group oppose each other, and enter situations of conflict, the group plays an important part. By having to consider other people's perspectives, input, and ideas, teens learn through their group membership that they are a part of a greater whole.

These conflicts might arise when the goals or behaviors of two or more individuals in the group—or between different groups—are incompatible. These conflicts can range from mild disagreements to physical fights.

> "Disagreements do not affect my relationships with other members. I am friends with all of them. I don't take sides in fights that may occur within the group."
>
> *Natalie, 17, Choir*

> "If another person from another group is doing something to me, I retaliate."
>
> *Dedric, 16, Gang*

Physical disputes rarely occur in more mainstream groups. Generally, most groups approach their conflicts with "ultimate good" for themselves and their group in mind. Admittedly, during the conflict itself this goal might not be so easy to discern.

Friendship and Power

When teenagers turn to their friends, they often seek out "positions of influence" with those friends. For some, subtle influences include having their friends in the group listen when they speak. Nodding and agreement might provide enough reinforcement. Other teenagers pursue power within their group by seeking office or a position of authority. Still others have the potential to demonstrate aggressiveness within the group. They do not create consensus nor encourage group-building. Instead, aggressors look out for themselves first, the group second. They destroy, rather than build. Fortunately, most groups recognize the negative impact such teenagers have, and exclude these members from participation.

When the group provides the positive reinforcement teenagers are seeking, the friendship will naturally follow. Power struggles usually slide into the distance, as teenagers seek to solidify their friendships—the purpose for the group in the first place.

Members of gangs and other antisocial groups look for different sources of friendship and power in their cliques. According to Ted, a former gang member:

> We need to be more realistic about our use of the word *power*. It involves more than real uses. It involves the perception of power within a given group or gang. Many personalities 'in the know' will tell us that the gangs provide a family unit, which is a big part of their recruitment strategies. This was not true for me, not the reason why my contemporaries and I joined a gang. We wanted

power. We wanted the power that being in the gang brought. . . . The power we felt in our guts when we walked down the street, to have citizens pull their small children and dogs indoors. We were in control. We had the power to create fear in others.

Teens Assert Themselves

Teenagers expend a substantial effort to "find themselves." A significant part of this struggle involves the search for control over their own destinies: the ability to determine their own fates for now and later. This, of course, requires teenagers to establish their identities as self-sufficient and able to handle the *authority* to make decisions that will work for them and others.

Part of mastering authority entails the teenager's willingness to reach beyond personal safety zones, to take risks—willingness to fail, to make mistakes, and to succeed. Such mastery means knowing that some questions do not have immediate answers.

Teenagers face a real dilemma by wanting to assert their own authority over their own lives. During adolescence, teens are still dependent on their parents for food, clothing, shelter, family support, and more. For most teens, these dependencies will probably continue until they reach adulthood and, for some, well into their adult years.

One immediate way teenagers handle their sense of help-lessness involves *back talk.* Responses like "In your face," "You don't know what you're talking about," and "Eat it" have worked their way into the day-to-day jargon of today's teenagers. This language prompts parental frustration and defensiveness.

Experts, however, say that teenagers, and even younger children, use language of the times to express their negative emotions. In the fifties, words like "damn" or "hell" would have prompted washing a child's mouth out with soap. Teenagers who talk back demonstrate a normal part of adolescent behavior. Often back talk helps teenagers spontaneously express their anger and frustration, especially when they sense that they have no other ways to handle their emotions. It can also help them gain power, attention, and identity.

According to many experts, parents should understand that back talk has replaced physical violence, for many teenagers, as a way of dealing with rage and disappointment. Cynthia Whitham, author of *Win the Whining War and Other Skirmishes: A Family Peace Plan* (Perspective Publishing, 1991), says that parents should not get "bent out of shape" by yelling, correcting, or punishing their teenagers just for the words they use. This just feeds the use of back talk, and helps ensure that such language becomes a habit. Parents should learn to weigh their discipline, to match the action. For example, parents will not give the same level of attention to back talk as to teenagers pounding on younger siblings or drinking and driving.

As parents work with their teenagers, they can help them learn positive ways to assert themselves. This assertiveness can enhance the teen's opportunities and desires to become a responsible adult.

Teens Emerge as Responsible Adults

Teenagers undergo a wide range of developmental challenges during adolescence. They experience:
- A personal revolution that has mandated a pulling-apart from their parents, at least for now.
- The evolution of their identities.
- The merging of their "being" with other teenagers who are experiencing the same developmental challenges.
- The influence of the group in their lives, and their influence on the group.

And now . . . teenagers approaching the end of their adolescence will take on new responsibilities. "Where do I go from here?" is a question most teens find themselves repeating, over and over again.

Mourning Lost Friendships

The loss or letting go of one friendship or many—the group—can create one of the most traumatic mourning periods in the life of a teenager. Friendship, at other times in our history, might have been considered less important than romantic love or family bonds. Today, however, the sense of dependency on friends and groups has taken a primary place in the lives of our nation's teenagers.

Most of contemporary literature addresses how to deal with the loss of lovers or parents or spouses. Teenagers will search a long time, and probably in vain, in their search for studies, research, and answers to handling the loss of a friend.

One friendship ending occurs through a gradual *growing apart*, like when one teenager moves away or goes to a different school. Even this separation, when prompted by reasons beyond the friendship, can cause particular pain for the person left behind.

"My first good friendship memory, since we moved here from England in 1981, was going trick-or-treating with all the new friends I met in our high-rise. The worst is when one of them, Adam, came to say good-bye, because his parents were moving to San Diego."

Reza, 16, Scholastic

"My earliest memories of friendship involved the boy down the street. We had great times digging in his sandbox and building forts together. He moved away after a few years. I missed him."

Jonathan, 17, Religious

"People change as they grow up and choose different roads. So, our friendships change. You will know some people whom you always want to be around and . . . others just once in awhile."

Paul, 19, Cultural

Another reason for the ending of friendship relates to *betrayal*. In many ways, this evokes the same feelings that the loss of a boyfriend or girlfriend might create. Examples of betrayal include:

- Being replaced by another person.
- Not being supported in times of need.
- Misuse and abuse of material belongings.
- Disrespect for the friend's personal ideas and beliefs.

Teenagers have the potential to experience many betrayals during adolescence. Each betrayal carries with it difficult memories, and lessons.

> "When we were younger we accepted each other. In high school, I was not the right religion to still be considered a good friend."
>
> *Africa, 19, Cultural*

> "Betrayal means arguments, rumors, and gossip."
>
> *Alyssa, 15, Letterman*

> "I learned about betrayal when my cousin died. I was very sad. Right then I knew that I wanted to go put 'in the dirt' whoever killed him."
>
> *Kiki, 14, Gang*

For teenagers, anger and sadness dominate as the two most common emotions they will experience when their friendships end. The depth of these emotions will depend on the nature and extent of the friendship. In the extreme, the break-up of some friendships will cause teenagers to experience all of the traumas of separation they might feel when separating from a parent or other family member.

Fortunately, for most teenagers, the separation from the group signals their emergence into a new stage of their lives. They might eventually "grow into" another group, or opt to solidify their individuality before aligning with the next group. Often, friendships from the group will remain important to the emerging adult—another plus of the group experience.

Beyond the Group

As teenagers move from adolescence into adulthood, separating from their historic support groups, finding their own identities . . . they often have their first look at a world larger than themselves.

On the verge of adulthood, older teenagers often experience their first opportunities to make an impact on the world-at-large. Their focus on the future takes on new importance. One of the primary activities they might engage in is *goal-setting*. They look ahead to their futures, and the impact they can make on their communities, on the world. Fortunately, the vast majority of teenagers get positive reinforcement at home. Seventy-five percent of HOBY participants said that their parents "give them positive strokes" in their personal goal-setting.

Possibly for the first time, older teenagers sit down to determine their preferences. They might even find themselves floating into a waking dream state. Good for them. This ability to ignore the can't-shouldn't-wouldn't restrictions that had directed them until this time in their lives will, at this juncture, become one of their greatest allies in self-accomplishment. . . . In determining where to go from here.

When older teenagers permit themselves to become unrestricted thinkers, they empower themselves to reach high, to achieve their personal aspirations. Ninety-four percent of HOBY respondents recognized their own "substantial influence on their own futures."

The ten most preferred descriptions, in order of priority, HOBY teens from outside the United States used to describe their futures were: *Success, happiness, family, bright, fulfilling, challenging, exciting, promising, fun*, and *work*. American teenagers described their personal futures, in order of descending preferred characterizations, as: *Successful, exciting, happy, bright, fulfilling, promising, positive, challenging, ambitious*, and *hopeful*. Neither list of top-ten descriptions includes the word "friend," perhaps because friendship is so integral to their lives, and dynamically influences every other description of their futures.

Teenagers—and the families who love and support them—need to learn to believe in their aspirations, in the power of their dreams. Based on dreams, some of the greatest personal achievements have occurred:

- The Englishman, with both legs amputated, who would not let other people tell him what he could not do. In 1989 I met this athlete when he won a gold medal, representing his country in world championship volleyball competition.
- The high school graduate who, in 1973, was a fast-food chain worker for two dollars an hour. In 1994, he owned forty-two restaurants.
- The accountant who could not get a job in his first fifty-two interviews. As an aspiring law student, he went to the only law school in the country that would accept him. He got a job with the only law firm in the country that would hire him. Ten years later, he owned his own law firm and personally makes more than ten million dollars each year.

What makes dreaming so important, anyway? For starters, teenagers do not have to make all of their dreams come true to experience the joy of personal fulfillment. Each dream unleashes its own excitement and reward, even when only partially experienced. This occurs because the dreamer—that teenager—owns the dream.

Sometimes, just thinking about the dream, and pursuing it, brings pleasure and personal satisfaction. The relationship teens have with their friends helps them reinforce their effort to plot and explore these dreams.

When their dreams do come true, adolescents enjoy the splendor of these personal achievements. They can reach within themselves to know that they excelled. With this soaring sense of personal achievement, teenagers often discover other benefits: sharing this personal success with their larger circle of friends, their group. As they look beyond themselves, during these tender-yet-tough years, teenagers learn to acknowledge the value of support and friendship. This fortification helps adolescents sustain their efforts to move forward, to make a positive difference in their lives and the lives of others. Teen and group: one plus one . . . success.

Quick Points

- The push and pull of the adolescent years often peaks with a *struggle for power*.
- Throughout their adolescence teenagers experience major adjustments to *authority*.
- Parents have the front-line position of authority in the lives of their teenagers.
- The style of parenting will determine the kind of relationship parents will have with their children. This ultimately affects the types of relationships teenagers have with their groups.
- A sample of parenting styles includes parents who are: *overcritical, combative, friendly, absent, authoritarian, outrageous*, and *responsible.*
- When parents deal with teenagers' negative behaviors, they have options. Most parents punish their teenagers for negative behavior.
- Punishment needs to be connected with the negative act so that the teenager can learn what not to do.
- Parents should consider alternatives for punishment. One of these alternatives enables teenagers to take responsibility for their actions. Another allows them to make amends.
- Other alternatives to punishment involve forms of *discipline*.
- Parents should broaden their focus beyond the negative activities of their teenagers. They need to invest more time, energy, and concern in their children's positive accomplishments.

- Parents should offer their children *praise,* whenever appropriate and possible.
- Praise helps parents *affirm* their teenager's positive behavior.
- Praise includes two parts: The parents' words and feelings, and the teenager's conclusions.
- Offering praise can create anxieties in teenagers, because it can set them up for future expectations.
- When teenagers experience the benefits of praise, they can transfer these good feelings to their group.
- Teenagers value their group behavior as one of the most enjoyable features of their teen years.
- Conflicts within the peer group usually only reach the level of oral disagreements. In antisocial groups, however, physical conflicts can occur.
- When teenagers turn to their friends, they often seek positions of influence with these friends.
- When the group provides positive reinforcement for their thoughts and actions, teenagers tend to experience enhanced friendships.
- Power struggles usually lessen as teenagers seek to solidify their friendships.
- Teenagers seek power of self, over self, in the pursuit of their own goals.
- Some teenagers use *back talk* to assert their identities with their parents and other adults.
- Teens often mourn lost friendships with the same intensity they would mourn the loss of family members.
- Friendships usually end through a natural *growing apart* or through *betrayal.*
- Often, as teenagers emerge into adulthood, they experience their first look at voluntary separation from peers.
- When older teenagers reach the end of adolescence, they might have their first experience at looking ahead and setting goals. Many learn to see beyond themselves for the first time.
- Teenagers—emerging adults—do not have to make all of their dreams come true to experience the joy of personal fulfillment.

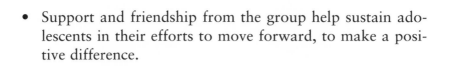

- Support and friendship from the group help sustain adolescents in their efforts to move forward, to make a positive difference.

Part 2
Getting Parents Involved

8

From Past to Present
The Role of the Family

Kenny walked into the kitchen. His stepmother was pouring hot chocolate into four mugs, one for each of the family's children: Kenny, his half-brother, Randy, and his two step-sisters, Linda and Sandy. Simultaneous dialogues bounced off the walls, the same way that sounds rebound at reunions of friends who have not seen each other for eons of time. No specific purpose prompted their morning conversations, sometimes just words. Breakfast drew into contact people who once were strangers—people whose lives had crossed each other's in such different ways, at different times.

The early friendship history of many of today's teenagers has been complicated in the past several years by changes in the American family. Teenagers have learned—or adapted to—the demand to grow up in new, more fluid living arrangements. These changed family arrangements can have some negative impact on adolescents. However, positive ones arise, too. Teenagers have new opportunities to exercise their independence and maturity. In addition, they have exposure to more adult role models.

Adolescence definitely challenges teenagers in their efforts to negotiate their way. Compounding this challenge, parents often fill this growth period with voices of disappointment in their teens. "Today's kids just don't measure up. . . ." "When I was a kid. . . ." "Children today just don't know how good they have it." Parents must realize the impact of these negative statements, especially when repeated often. Teenagers already struggle with their vulnerabilities, and negative parental "charges"—stated again and again—only serve to compound the adolescent struggle. In addition, such negativity will naturally influence the teens' subsequent attitudes and actions.

A Look Back

The contrasts between parents and teens have long histories. Such sage influences as Aristotle, Shakespeare, and Mark Twain have addressed the subject of teens and their adjustments with the universal message: "We can hardly wait until they grow up."

Parents and society expect teens to make many serious adjustments during adolescence. Part 1 of this book addressed several of these matters, and teens efforts to:

- Establish a strong sense of identity, self-esteem, and self-worth.
- Develop self-sufficiency and independence from their parents and other adults who influence them.
- Create and nurture positive relationships with their friends, their groups.
- Learn how to meet the challenges of stress and pressure to survive and surpass.
- Decide on their futures and begin taking steps toward achieving them.

To understand better our nation's attitudes toward its teenagers, let's take a more detailed look at the evolution of the family.

The Premodern Family

Adolescence, as we know it today, is a relatively new phenomenon. We need only look back to the beginning of the twentieth century to discover some of the major influences that created changes in our teens.

Prior to this time, adolescents were considered miniature adults. At early ages, they labored at adult tasks—whether they be work assignments or farm chores. Their parents expected them to contribute economically to bolster the family welfare. As future providers, teenagers also represented security for their parents in old age. To help assure this, parents—especially fathers—had a significant influence over the selection of their children's spouses.

No one recognized childhood and adolescence as "stages" of growing up. Parents treated childhood merely as a period that marked the end of apprenticeship and the beginning of adult work.

In early American families, the father prevailed as the child-rearer. He instilled in the family's children their values, religious beliefs, standards, and morals. He also served as their primary teacher for basic skills like reading and writing.

Premodern families consisted of the nuclear family, but often older generations did not live with them. Why? They often did not live long enough. Also, members of families usually spent their entire lives in the same community, surrounded by people they had always known. This fortified the sense of identity and the need for security that teenagers, later in history, would struggle to secure for themselves.

With the change from agrarian lifestyles to the industrialization of America, families experienced widespread separations nationwide. For the first time, fathers travelled into the cities to work, thus relinquishing some of their parental duties. Mothers' roles took on new levels of importance in child-raising. It took until the mid-nineteenth century for mothers to be identified as the full-time care-giver for the home and children.

The actual make-up of the family also began to change during the nineteenth century. Married couples reduced the numbers of their offspring from seven or eight to three or four. Children themselves took on new identities. Rather than being viewed as economic arms of the family, children and adolescents took on the image of innocents.

The Modern Family

In America, the modern concept of adolescence originated in the early 1900s. At this time, compulsory education was required until age sixteen, child labor legislation appeared, and the juvenile justice system emerged. Parents and other adults discovered a need to redefine the boundaries between childhood, adolescence, and adulthood. Possibly, for the first time, parents and other adults understood that adolescence was actually a distinct period of a person's life. Parents began to recognize that they needed to handle adolescence with the same respect as any other stage of life.

Jumping into the second half of the twentieth century, the 1950s thrived on the concept of the family as married couples who had children. The child-bearing rate was unusually high by twentieth-century standards, with the baby boom peaking in 1957. The divorce rate was unusually low. Also, during the 1950s, women married earlier than they did twenty years before or after. Possibly, the war experience inspired a renewed sense of family.

In the 1960s, expectations took a roller-coaster ride. Adults who became fathers and mothers had high expectations, and developed a strong taste for material goods. One victim of this thinking was the family. Divorce, and the onslaught of single-parent families, skyrocketed. For many, during this time of liberation and freedom-seeking, divorce represented flights into independence.

During the 1970s, rates for marriage and births slipped to an all-time low. Adults delayed marriages for many reasons: More women in the workplace becoming economically independent, the availability of newfound contraceptive options, and the Vietnam War.

Change became the watchword for the status of the family during the 1980s. The work force grew in leaps and bounds with mothers of infants—the teenagers of the nineties. These working mothers, with the stresses of working and motherhood, faced the need to stretch the boundaries of family to accommodate the dual demands. Fathers also experienced change, resulting from their expanded roles in parenting. The impact on their children: change and stress.

This evolutionary process has produced another by-product that directly impacts today's adolescents. They must adjust to many more "family settings" in their lives than their parents did. Many of these settings have nothing to do with the biological family. Confused and insecure, many of these teenagers turn to their friends—their groups—for the continuity and support of "family."

The Contemporary Family

Parents have never been so stretched in the demands for their time and their presence. Work, family, and whatever else might make claim. Fortunately, most parents realize that they need to adjust to these changes and demands.

Although they are spending less time with their children, most parents are working with a vengeance, and a powerful consciousness, to help their offspring adjust to these changes. This parenting consciousness may never have had such a presence in this nation. Adults realize that parenthood is no longer based on economics or dependencies. Rather, most parents now have children because they want them.

Because parenthood is optional, parents have choices about how they will handle their responsibilities. This includes everything from problem solving to emotional support to listening. Put simply, modern parenting and modern adolescence, combined, comprise a new national experience in personal development and relationship-building.

Impact of Divorce

Unfortunately, these same modern times impose stresses that many parents strive to overcome. Pressures directly impact their adolescents. Divorce. Statistics bear out that about one-half of today's marriages will end in divorce. This means that only half of today's children live in "traditional nuclear families"—with dad at work, and mom making a full-time commitment to raising the family. Millions of the children of divorce are adolescents. Twenty-five percent of the children today will live with a step-parent before reaching the age of sixteen. One-third will live in single-parent families, usually with mom as the head of the household.

Broken families, blended families, single-parent families, and joint-custody families create challenges for both fathers and mothers. These parents can generally look to their own parents for positive parental role modeling, with family as a center of focus. Therefore, today's parents often have no one to teach them about part-time parenting and part-time adolescent-rearing.

In addition to the stresses of changed families, parents and their children will probably undergo economic changes. Sometimes, teens must take on jobs to assist their families, or their families move to new homes and neighborhoods. These changes produce upheavals in the family when adolescents are already struggling with internal and external dilemmas that accompany their adolescent revolution. More than ever, parents need to provide support to their teens during these transitions.

> "I adjust my thinking to help her as she changes and grows rapidly through this transition to adulthood."
> *Barbara, Mother*
> *Mary, 16, SADD*

> "I recognize the importance of just 'being there' to support and encourage her choices to be a responsible adult."
> *Sandy, Mother*
> *Jasmine, 16, Scholastic*

Parents often use periods of loss as times for readjustments with their children, especially adolescent children. Some parents seek to redefine their identities and experience newfound independence, sometimes excluding their children in the process. Others explore new alternatives for relationships and possible support. Still others turn to their teens for friendship and companionship.

While adolescents are trying to figure out who they are, parents sometimes expect their teens to learn about the "new people" they—the parents—are becoming. For families in which remarriage occurs, teens also must learn the identities of step-parents, and step-siblings. At the very least, this produces awesome expectations. Equally significant, as adolescents are learning their new "roles," so are their step-parents. One important rule can help step-parents ease part of the stress: Step-parents are not replacements—they are additions.

Moving Forward in New Directions

As the nature of the family continues to evolve, parents and their adolescent children will take on new identities and responsibilities. Their expectations of each other will also mature. One of the major factors affecting their relationship involves outsiders: friends—the group the teenager selects to provide identity and support. To help parents understand the group-selection process, I wrote Part 1 of this book. I have designed Part 2 to take readers to the next level: Getting parents positively involved in the group-selection process.

Quick Points

- The early friendship history of many of today's teenagers has been complicated by changes in the American family.
- Adolescence has always been a difficult time for teenagers to negotiate.
- Disparities between parents and teens have long histories.
- Prior to the twentieth century, parents and society treated adolescents as miniature adults.
- In early American families, fathers exercised the predominant parenting role.
- In America, the modern concept of adolescence originated in the early 1900s.
- Beginning with the second half of the twentieth century, the status of the family changed. More mothers went to work, fathers' and mothers' roles changed, and the concept of family took on new and diverse meanings.

- Friends and groups have become more important for today's adolescents, because the nature of the family and the family setting have changed so dramatically.
- Contemporary parents have greater choices than ever before about family. For the first time in history, parents are having children, not to boost the family economically but because they want them.
- Divorce substantially impacts families. About half of today's marriages end in divorce. Only about one-half of today's children, millions of whom are teenagers, live in "nuclear" families. Twenty-five percent of today's children will live with a step-parent before the age of sixteen.
- Parents and their children experience significant periods of adjustment because of divorce. Roles and expectations of teenagers dramatically change, especially because teenagers are already involved in the search for their own identities.

9
The Ties That Bind

When her daughter, Tina, was younger, Krista took her everywhere. No matter where their journeys about town routed them, even strangers would point to the mother-daughter duo and comment: "How adorable, they're so much alike." Mom and daughter dressed in similar colors and fashions, wore their hair the same way, laughed at the same silly jokes, and even shared secrets. "You'll always be my best friend, Mommy," Tina would whisper to her mother. This promise faded quickly, if not completely, when Tina moved into her teen years.

Many of the expectations, then disappointments, parents experience with their teenagers go far beyond that particular parent-child relationship. Often, the ways parents deal with their teenagers are colored by the parents' feelings about themselves and their own lives. For some parents, *dis*colored paints a more accurate picture.

Parents have a way of using their children's development as markers for their own. Their teen's emergence into adolescence can symbolize the parents' own stepping into a stage of life they might not be prepared to accept—middle age. So, in the spirit of adjustment, this time can require both parents and their children to deal with stages of their lives that demand change, and acceptance.

These simultaneous realignments might confuse both parents and their adolescents, especially when neither understands what the other is encountering. Helplessness.

Each can bring out the worst in the other, with much more frequency than bringing out the best. Frustration.

Parents and teens expect so much, often too much, from each other. Disappointment.

Fortunately, knowing that parents and teens are working their ways through parallel universes can launch the journey toward a generational reunion. To reach this elevated relationship between parent and child, parents first need to understand in more detail the parent-teen relationship.

From Parent to Child, to Child . . .

Most parents can look back on their own childhoods and remember personal promises to themselves: "I will never treat my children the way my parents treat me—never." Yet, in the moments requiring discipline, these same parents often find themselves repeating almost the identical words and actions as their parents: "You're grounded for the rest of your life." "If you talk on the phone one more time when you should be doing your homework, I'll have it disconnected." "No more allowance for you until you can learn to be responsible with your money."

Or, they might use the same consoling language in times requiring comfort. "Let Mommy give you a hug and make it all better." "That's okay, son, you played the best game you could." "Mom and Dad will always be here when you need to talk."

The best intentions of parents often become the best intentions of their children, and *their* children—a cycle: old habits in new generations.

Multigenerational Baggage

Each generation brings with it a load of baggage that represents not only the myths and expectations of that generation, but all those that preceded it: religion, morality, ethics, even friendship-formation, and more. This happens because parents often do not resolve their own conflicts or form their own independent identities before they become parents themselves.

As a natural course of action for this unfinished business parents pass on to their children not only ideas, but also unresolved personal conflicts. The degree to which people accept and pass on ideas from their parents will depend on how well they have developed their own identities, separate and apart from their parents.

> "My parents set positive examples by having good friends in their lives who were good people. They wanted me to learn by my own mistakes about what to believe. They let me know when they really liked my friends a lot, even do today!"
>
> *Judy, Step-Mother*
> *Alyse, 13, Music*

Even extreme efforts to create separate identities can reflect strong ties with parents. For example, when children imitate their parents, they naturally feel connected with them. At the other extreme, when children rebel against their parents, for the sake of being different, they are still tied to their parents by the act of rebellion. True freedom allows children to enjoy similarities and differences with their parents . . . to recognize their own individual identities and choices in either situation.

The model remains: We repeat with our children the patterns we learned as children. Parents find comfort in repeating what they know—the parenting styles used on them. This empowers these parents to search into their own pasts to find answers they could not have known as children. Maybe, with a second experience, all of their own parents' behaviors will finally make sense.

Sometimes, however, this loyalty to parents and their parenting methods does not work with today's teenagers. Changed times, changed attitudes, changed families. Parents might often wonder if anything of their past remains the same. At least their memories survive. Parents need to remember, however, that the past they own belongs to them. The present should be tempered with learning—an opportunity to unfold—for their teenagers. Their teens need to live their own experiences, to make their own mistakes, to build their own memories.

> "I do try to influence my daughter—probably too much. I think my standards may be too high. I am trying to keep my mouth shut, to allow her some unpleasant experiences if she needs them. Generally, I trust her intuition about life."
>
> *Barbara, Mother*
> *Mary, 16, SADD*

Teenagers should not be loaded to the brim with generations of guilt and unrealistic expectations. They should be allowed, and encouraged, to travel their journey with lightly loaded backpacks, seasoned with their parents' teachings and support.

Reducing Expectations and Raising Returns

Often parental expectations of their teen's behavior create block walls between parent and child. Sometimes, these expectations mirror the parent's own unfulfilled personal dreams, or they represent the parent's hopes for "a better life for my child than I had." Whatever the reason, parents historically have set *levels of performance* for their children. Teenagers often respond with: "Whose life is this, anyway?"

Lofty expectations can poison the parent-teen relationship. By the time the teenager reaches the age of actual performance, parents' expectations often have swollen so greatly that no teenager would be able to fulfill the dream.

Sadly, the disparity between parental expectation and teen performance can also produce disappointment—for parent and child. So, even when parents do praise their children, these teenagers might ask themselves and their parents:

- "Will you *ever* be pleased with what I do? Or . . . just keep pushing me?"
- "Have you ever thought that I don't want to live my life for you?"

- "Is my success important because I did something great, or because it makes you look good?"

Parents should be committed to valuing their teens for who they already are, not for who they might become. They should seek and find opportunities to cheer on their teens. Anything teens do, by themselves or with their friends, reflects their efforts to create their own identities.

Where a teenager goes helps define *identity*. The teenager's effort—*how hard* that teenager tries—reflects *self-reliance*. Each of these factors includes a push-pull situation for parent and child. They represent parents' efforts to keep their children within their own wing span, and teenagers' own efforts to fly free and far.

Acceptance

Parents can help themselves break away from the multigenerational load they have been carrying. This does not discount all of the wisdom and sage counsel their parents and *their* parents have shared with them. It just creates a process to ease the burden of expectations and directives for future generations. A few suggestions to parents of adolescents:

- *Accept that your own childhood is past.* You survived the same experiences that your teens are now living, day by day. However, because you have survived, you are in charge of your life now. You need not turn to the past itself, or any particular person from your past, to cast blame or responsibility for what you are doing with your life today. This should provide a substantial source of relief and freedom.
- *Acknowledge that your parents gave it their best effort.* You might have trouble with the memories of how your parents raised you. You might have complaints about why they made the decisions they made, and how they faced family challenges on a daily basis. In reality, your parents did the best job they knew how to do in rais-

ing you. They brought to their child-raising experience all that their parents gave them in terms of memories and sage advice. Probably, too, they made a few original decisions-of-the-day along the way. Now it's your turn.

• *Applaud your parents for giving you life.* At times, you might ask why on earth your parents ever decided to have you, and wish that they had decided otherwise. However, when all of your problems shake loose, you probably recognize the miracle of life, and that they created the miracle that became your life. Even if these are not the same parents who raised you—whoever you consider your "parents" to be—they have contributed to the person you have become. They have added something each day, if only through lessons of long ago, to define the composite person you are right now. This alone gives reason to celebrate!

Once parents accept that they can and should unload the personal and familial baggage that they have been carrying, they can take a very healthy step forward. This movement will help enrich their relationship with their teens and the people their teens select as friends.

Just Who Are We, Anyway?

To make progress in the parent-teen relationship, both must first define the scope of the "we" in their bond. How much should parent and child *combine* their energies, thoughts, and activities to form a working relationship?

One ongoing source of union should involve *mutual respect*. Parents need to respect their children in the same ways they ask their children to respect them. This should not imply that teens are necessarily *equal* in every aspect of the family. Parents have certain responsibilities that must prevail: Providing security and basic-needs resources, setting rules, making final decisions that impact the entire family . . . . However, when possible, parents should "partner" with their teens. Parents should learn to listen without judgment, and encourage input and feedback from their teens in the same way these parents would have hoped for themselves during adolescence.

Parents also need to provide *nurturance* for their children. Parents must give their teens the emotional life support that will reinforce their healthy mental, physical, and emotional growth.

Some sociologists say that planned one-to-one activities, maybe weekly or monthly, will reinforce the relationship between the parent and the child. This would be a special time they own together. When the solidity of the relationship is shared, many teenagers often want to expand their involvement to include their friends from the group. It can be healthy for parents and teens to enlarge the circle when the teenager suggests it.

> "I want to know who their friends are. My part-time job allows me to work around a lot of teenagers. I like to interact with them as an adult. I don't try to be a teenager."
>
> *Karen, Mother*
> *Don, 17, Key Club*

> "Interaction is important, though I know not to be overly involved or over-bearing. I encourage my son to introduce his friends to me. We all do scouting activities together. We're on a first-name basis."
>
> *Ray, Father*
> *Ray Jr., 13, Boy Scouts*

> "I attend school plays and dance performances. We go shopping and eat out weekly. We sew prom dresses, create crafts, and bake cookies. We make popcorn and watch horror movies. I get invited to school dances to chaperon. Our home is always open to her friends."
>
> *Sandy, Mother*
> *Lisa, 16, Leadership*

Sometimes teenagers might get heavily involved with group activities. At other times, they might preempt plans with their parents to "hang out" with their friends. Parents often take these actions personally, feeling rejected. Even offended. At this stage of their lives, however, teenagers do not always look at the far-reaching impacts of their behaviors. They focus on the "now" of their decisions. By understanding this predisposition, parents should be able to ease their sensitivities, and put into proper perspective, their teens' spontaneous actions.

Of course, this "irresponsibility" can especially unnerve parents when the activity involves tickets to a Metallica concert or a weekend away in the mountains. If the teenager repeats this last-minute thinking often enough, it can reinforce a self-centered habit. Parents have a right, and an obligation, to tell the teen: "We need to talk about something that is bothering us." Then, the parents can assertively address the issue using the four-part formula I described in chapter 3: "When you-I feel-because-I prefer."

When teens substitute planned family activities with unplanned, impromptu fun with their friends, parents can also offer their teens a different shared activity. Parents can suggest alternatives.

Rebalancing the Family

As children become parents and older parents become grandparents, opportunities for rebalancing the family can take shape. Conservatively, these times of passing the torch between parent and child, and child . . . serve as crucial transitions between the generations. They help redefine the roles and relationships between the generations. They also influence the relationships between siblings of the same generation.

Of course, how well a family adjusts to each transition between parents and children will depend on how well the generation that preceded it did. The success of adjustment will also vary according to how well each generation redefined the rules.

Each generation enjoys the possibility for new freedoms and new adventures. As each previous boundary is expanded or removed, the possibilities for the newest generation increase.

However, defining and redefining the parameters for each generation requires that parents and their children recognize just how interdependent they really are.

Unfortunately, during the 1990s, parents and their children have been "losing touch with one another," according to Secretary of Education Richard Riley. During a 1994 presentation to national educators attending a conference at Georgetown University (Associated Press, February 16, 1994), Riley launched a "family involvement campaign." He stressed his concern about America's children.

> If I am troubled by anything it is this: We seem, as a nation to be drifting toward a new concept of childhood, which says that a child can be brought into this world and allowed to fend for himself or herself.

How can we reconnect America's children with their parents? It must start with parents, and in the beginning of the parent-child relationship. In the early stages, parents need to realize that, with their children, they are not equals, nor can they be friends. The parent must prevail, at least during the earlier years. However, once parents and their children physically separate—when the child has become an adult—relationship equality has a much greater chance for success and survival.

Ironically, when children learn to respect and value their parents and *their* parents for who they are, these teens have taken the first step toward their own identity. Learning how to respect others serves as an anchor to their understanding themselves and their own friends.

Quick Points

- Often the ways that parents deal with their children is colored, or *dis*colored, by their relationships with their own parents, and . . . *their* parents . . . .
- Parents have a way of using their children's development as markers for their own.

- Most parents remember childhood promises they made to themselves *not* to raise *their* children the same way that they were raised.
- Each generation inherits the multigenerational "baggage" of the generations that preceded it.
- One child-raising model remains between generations: Parents tend to repeat with their children the patterns they learned from how their parents treated them.
- Often, parents' expectations of their teenagers' behavior can create a block wall between the parents and their teens.
- Sometimes, parents' expectations mirror their own unfulfilled dreams.
- Parents have historically set *levels-of-performance* standards for their children.
- Parents should value their teens for who they already are, not for who they might become.
- Parents should:
  - ← Accept that their own childhoods have passed.
  - ← Acknowledge that their parents gave them their best efforts.
  - ← Applaud their parents for giving them life.
- Progress in the parent-teen relationship requires defining the scope of the "we" in the relationship.
- One ongoing source of union between parent and teen is *mutual* respect.
- Parents should recognize their responsibility to provide *nurturance* to their teens.
- Planned one-to-one activities can also enhance relationship-building between parent and teen.
- Parents need to be flexible with their teens and shared activities, because teens tend to think in the "now" of their lives and change plans quickly.
- Opportunities to *rebalance* families occur when new generations reach decision-making stages.
- Because many situations require parents to prevail, it is difficult for parents and their children—even their teens—to be equals.

10
Opening the Lines

Friday night. The dialogue, seemingly set on "replay," echoes a conversation voiced almost every weekend since the Bentons' seventeen-year-old son, Greg, started high school. "What's it going to take for you to let me take the car to the game?" Greg asks his parents.

"We don't want you driving alone at night, especially when you have to go out of town," his parents respond in a near-whisper, avoiding eye contact with their son.

"I drive safely and have never gotten into trouble," Greg pleads.

"You know how we feel." They remain in their chairs, settled across the living room from where Greg is standing.

"Tell me why you don't trust me," the teenager queries.

"We have our reasons and feel better when you do what we say," Mr. Benton says, with his eyes focused on the headlines of the evening newspaper. Mrs. Benton has returned to her computer in the den.

"Here we go again. Do you *ever* listen to me?" Greg blurts out, as he exits the house, car keys in hand.

To understand the communication process—with its successes and its failures—families need to learn some key communication basics. To help parents set the right example as effective communicators, I will explain several principles that I have taught during the past three decades. Many of these "lessons" result directly from my own mistakes. So I am pleased to pass on a little wisdom to help parents who read this material learn without having to stumble. These principles apply in most communication situations. Although I will focus on how parents can use these skills with their teenagers, I strongly believe that parents must develop and apply these communication skills long before their children reach adolescence.

To ensure this learning process, parents should practice these *constructive communication* techniques regularly, and often. Through constructive communication—both as senders and receivers—parents can improve interactions with their teenagers.

Parents will define for themselves why they want to master communication excellence. Whatever the reasons both parents and adolescents will benefit from effective communications.

Body Talk

Communication begins well before the first word is spoken. It starts with *body language*. Through body talk—*non*verbal communication—parents make their initial impression on adolescents within the first three to seven seconds! Yes, it only takes a quick look to register an impression in another person's mind. In fact, research shows that in the average American family, as much as eighty percent of all communication is nonverbal. Rather than flinch at this reality, parents have the chance to put communication to work for themselves and their teenagers. Of course, the same principles will help teenagers with their parents!

No one is born with a natural style for body talk. All of us learn it in early childhood, and it accounts for fifty-five percent of a parent's communication with other people. Body language conveys meaning to others through emotions and feelings, not through mind-power or intellect. Body talk involves the speaker and listener in subtle ways. It includes facial expressions, hand gestures, body postures, use of space, and much more.

Facial Expressions

Facial expressions tell teenagers *how their parents feel*. Positive facial expressions include smiling or, at least, not scowling. An "open face" will convey a thousand unspoken messages to the teenager. A smile can help parents break through otherwise impenetrable barriers with their adolescents. However, they should remember to smile only when appropriate.

Certainly, parents will want to avoid frowning or scowling when their teenager is talking. Without speaking any words, negative facial expressions convey the idea of disagreement or disapproval, even dislike for their teenager. The easiest rule for parents to follow is: Have an open face whenever possible, but avoid the "happy look" when it conflicts with what they are saying or hearing.

For example, when Ron arrived home from a championship baseball game, in which he struck out twice, he needed some physical and emotional cooling-off time. Instead, as soon as he entered the house, his dad greeted him with his movie-star smile, gave him a hug, and remarked, "That was the worst game you ever played," and meant it. In this case, if his dad wanted to convey parental support during a rough time, his gestures alone could have made a positive, loving difference to Ron. However, the conflict between the positive gestures— nonverbal language—and negative words—verbal language—produced remorse in Ron.

Gestures

Gestures tell teenagers *what parents mean*. Positive hand and arm movements help speaking parents convey positive messages, without ever uttering a word. For instance, parents can use open-hand gestures to describe how they want to include their teenagers in an activity. Or, they can stand with unfolded arms to avoid giving the impression that they are "closing out" their teenagers.

Head movement also needs to support their words. When parents shake their heads left to right, yet say, "We really believe what you're saying," what are they really "saying" with their back-and-forth head movement? They are giving a mixed message, through conflicting words and gestures, and creating confusion for their teenager.

Touching can also influence the message. When parents want to "connect" with their teens, they can accomplish this effectively through a gentle touch or pat. Hugs work, too. This gentle physical contact should convey the message of caring—from parent to child. It can also help parents show respect for their teens.

> "I encourage my son in ways he understands and appreciates: Hugs, handshakes, and high-fives."
>
> *Ray, Father*
> *Ray Jr., 13, Boy Scouts*

Posture

Posture defines for teenagers *how much esteem parents have*. It also demonstrates what parents think about themselves in their teenager's presence. Teens pick up on their parents' posturing, even when it is subtle. Parents give a positive impression when they stand straight, not stiff, with their feet positioned under their shoulders. However, if this posture reflects too much "militarism," teens will pick up on the stiffness and often withdraw or pull back from their parents. This withdrawal can spur distancing.

Posture also includes the ways parents sit and walk, and in different environments. Each parent will want to ask: "What impression do I want to make? How do I want my teenager to think about me?" Parents have the ability to control these messages by the ways they carry themselves around their teens and their teens' friends.

Use of Space and Eye Contact

The use of personal space demonstrates *where parents feel comfortable*. It defines their own personal territories. It tells how much room parents require, or prefer, to ensure feelings of ease about who they are and what they do. For example, parents might feel comfortable sitting next to their teenage son's best friend in a movie theater. However, if they sit next to a group of unknown teenagers, they would probably feel easier about sitting with an empty seat between them.

Eye contact tells adolescents *how much their parents want to connect.* It clearly conveys the level of familiarity parents will share with their teens—their willingness to let their teenagers get close to them. Many experts agree that eye contact serves as one of the most powerful sources of nonverbal body talk. For first "connections" with their adolescents in a dialogue, parents should hold their eye contact for five to seven seconds. Any longer than that, without a momentary break in eye contact, might give the teenager an impression of parental aggression or hostility. Less than that can convey parental weakness.

More than a Whisper

Voice conveys thirty-eight percent of the communicated message. Talking on the phone bumps that percentage up to eighty-seven percent of a speaking parent's impact conveyed by voice.

So what does "voice" mean, anyway? It includes the vocal pitch, as well as volume, rate, diction, resonance, rhythm, and range. It also involves enthusiasm and conviction.

Here are a few tips for parents to develop effective use of voice. They should:

- Enunciate words clearly.
- Breathe normally. Speak in short, normal sentences so that they do not run out of breath.
- Speak pleasantly, with tonal variety, voice inflection, and comfortable rhythm.
- Avoid rushing. They need to give listeners a fair chance to absorb their message.
- Project, not shout, nor whisper.

Equally important, not using the voice at certain times will help parents deliver strong impressions. Pausing and breathing facilitate communications between parents and teens.

Words

Because body talk comprises fifty-five percent of a parent's communication, and voice accounts for thirty-eight percent, this leaves seven percent for the words themselves. Although the percentages are low, words constitute a crucial part of the message. They account for the distinction between languages, between cultures, between messages understood and messages lost.

When parents put words into action, their words should make sense in the context of their messages. Short words usually work best. Parents might think that they can impress their teenagers by using long words. Elaborate language might work for them in other environments. At home, these words might only impress—or even reach—the parent. Teenagers appreciate and respond best to words that "get to the point."

To be effective, these words should "paint pictures." Active words, colorful words, and words that other people can "see" when they are spoken will serve parents best. Such visual words also deliver clear messages, drive home important points, and cut out excessive or meaningless talk.

Parents should remember to speak in the "spoken word." They should not get distracted with the idea that important conversations between parent and child must sound like "declarations" or "recitations" of great pieces of literature. Nor should communications sound like something straight out of Bartlett's Quotations.

Parents should also learn—and teach their children—to feel comfortable with—and use frequently—"feeling" words. Words such as *angry, happy, sad, eager, disappointed, hurt, excited,* and *confused* encourage family members to express their emotions with each other. This language will help parents and teens make irreplaceable connections.

As far as other words are concerned, parents will benefit from learning the language their teenagers use to express themselves. Of course, these word choices will vary from region to region, city to city, and even neighborhood to neighborhood. One caution: Parents should not personally adopt their teens' language to impress their teens. They should learn the language to communicate with their teens, to understand the messages their teens are conveying.

Effective communications, from parent to teen, do not use or require teen "jargon." For example:

- "I'd like to talk with you. Is this a good time?
- "I know that I can count on you to make a good decision."
- "I don't necessarily approve of what you're doing, but I love you, anyway."
- "I know that you're getting older, and respect how you're developing. This is why I want to talk with you, not dictate to you."
- "I've considered what you've told me, and I don't think you are ready to leave town for the weekend with your friends. Please tell me why you feel I should say 'yes.' "

Teens will probably expect their parents to do more than just use the right words. They want their parents to absorb meanings, to respond to ideas, and to follow up with appropriate actions. To teenagers, communication involves more than just words. They mandate an ongoing process—a testing ground—for parents to show honest involvement with their children.

> "I talk with them, both jokingly and seriously. I also give advice when asked. I play games with them, and take them on trips. I strive to be very open and honest with them, and their friends."
>
> *Steven, Father*
> *Kansa, 17, Scholastic*

Wear Your Confidence

With all of these great recommendations imprinted on the mind, readers might be asking, "And how long do I have to learn all of this stuff?" The answer is simple. It requires a lifetime of learning. However, no one has to wait to benefit from this education in communications excellence. At this very moment, parents reading this chapter can *wear confidence* with power. Even if it takes a while to master communication skills, parents can still communicate effectively right now.

The process starts by developing a positive attitude—toward themselves as people and parents—and toward their adolescents. This will assist parents in making valuable impressions that can influence their teenagers. Parents can enhance this realm of influence by practicing the communication skills discussed earlier in this chapter. Teenagers will take their cues from self-confident parents and how they respond before even a word is uttered.

Humor also serves as a tremendous ally. Parents should avoid taking too many matters too seriously. Teenagers appreciate their parents' ability to laugh and smile. This can break a lot of tension. Parents do need to recognize, however, when and when not to incorporate humor in the communications. Humor can also succeed at turning negative situations into positive ones—whether the parent or the teenager initiates it.

Consider Dustin, who could be the offspring of any parent reading this book. Dustin often found himself in history class with classmates who got too serious about what he considered irrelevant subjects. He knew they would question the placement of commas in an insignificant document, but would never get to the impact of international treaties before the bell rang. So, one day he decided to take a stand, literally. Dustin retrieved his black marking pen, wrote a quick message on notepaper, and stood beside his desk. He raised the paper and, with a playful expression on his face, read its announcement aloud, "On Strike Against Historic Commas and Other Lost Causes."

Written Communication

Having learned ways to master the key elements in verbal and nonverbal communications, parents might want to move on to written communications. These skills can help parents make positive points with their teenagers. Why? Often, parents and teens have difficulty in communicating their ideas and needs orally. When this happens, written communications can make the needed connection in a timely fashion. Employers recognize the value of writing competence. Across the country, nearly ninety percent of this nation's employers consider writing skills as one of the most important requirements for productivity, career development, and promotion.

Parents and their teens can fine-tune their written messages to each other by considering a few tips. Parents should:

- Get to the point.
- Consider what is important to the teenager reading their message. First and foremost, they need to address their teen's interests.
- Use words their adolescents will understand.
- Be themselves and write in a natural, articulate style that feels comfortable to them.
- Use proper grammar, spelling, and sentence structure to convey their thoughts (but not to the extent that the drive for correctness outweighs the message).
- Favor subject-verb-object sentence forms.
- Introduce only one main idea per sentence.
- Avoid writing complicated, lengthy sentences when shorter, simpler ones will work. In fact, the American Press Institute studied how the length of sentences affects a reader's level of understanding. Readers will understand ninety percent of a message if the sentence is nineteen words or fewer. When the length climbs to twenty-five words, the level of understanding falls to sixty-four percent. At thirty words, the writer can expect only a thirty-four percent level of understanding.
- Vary the length of sentences. Include variety, some short

sentences and some longer sentences. The varying sentence-lengths will keep the teenager interested. Again, parents should remember to keep sentences an "understandable" length. One exception: When the meaning would be impaired by breaking the sentence into two or more, shorter ones.

- Use concise, short words when possible, by writing with descriptive words.
- Add "visual excitement" to the message. "Word pictures" should involve the teenager.
- Write with active verbs whenever possible.
- Avoid overuse of adverbs and adjectives. When parents use too many, or use them inappropriately, the message hits overload and misses the intended point.
- Write to *express* ideas, not to *impress* their teenager.

Assertive Behavior: The Source of Personal Power

When parents first learned about the need for effective communications with their teens, they probably focused on ways to get their points across firmly and quickly. However, the parenting experience has taught most parents to want and expect more of their communication exchanges with their teens. Beyond the mere communication of ideas, parents also want to feel positive about what they say and do. They also probably hope that their teenagers will respond to them with respect for what they say and how they convey it. To accomplish these twin goals, parents must *assert* themselves.

Assertive behavior will help parents promote mutual respect in their relationships with their children, and the earlier they develop these skills with their children, the better. Together, they will have the opportunity to develop *balanced communications* so that each of them can prosper from their interactions.

Assertiveness helps parents act in their own best interests, without being afraid to do so. It also helps them express their feelings to their teenagers honestly and comfortably. Parents can learn to trust their abilities to make positive decisions that affect the present and the future, both for themselves and their teenagers. However, if these decisions do not turn out the way parents expect, they can learn to make the needed changes.

Assertiveness also allows parents to ask for help, without feeling stupid or diminished. It empowers them to express their opinion or say 'no' without being concerned about fear or anxiety. Assertive parents will stand up for their rights without preventing their teenagers from enjoying their own rights. This empowerment provides parents with control over their lives, while not imposing excessive personal decisions on their teenagers. Forceful parents can discern when they should give their teens the room to make choices for themselves. In turn, they can help empower their teenagers to develop their own assertiveness.

> "I am a good communicator, because I care. I am always there for them, and am not afraid to try new angles if something isn't working."
>
> *Sandra, Mother*
> *Amber, 14, Social*

> "I'm not afraid to preach, when necessary. But I'm also willing to hear their point-of-view."
>
> *Karen, Mother*
> *Don, 17, Key Club*

Our culture reinforces assertive behavior because it is self-fulfilling, honest, and positively focused. Assertive parents work to build and enhance themselves and their families. Assertiveness, in both verbal and nonverbal communications, results in positive self-affirmations. These skills not only help the parents but their adolescents as well. This is not a universal behavior. It calls for judgments as distinctive as each parent and each situation. Assertive parents need to be socially responsible.

Assertive Communication

The ability for parents to express themselves effectively is one of their most basic parental needs. We learned earlier in this chapter that the how of expression will far outweigh the what of the message. Therefore, parents will want to learn how to effect nonverbal and verbal assertiveness through body posture, gestures, facial expressions, distance and physical connectedness, eye contact, and vocal qualities.

Some parents recognize that they want to develop more assertive behaviors with their teens through effective communications. Most teenagers eagerly express their preferences for parental behavior. From teens to parents:

- "Stop pressuring us to achieve all of the time."
- "Praise us when we do something well."
- "Tell us you love us, even if we act like we don't want to hear it."
- "Express yourselves honestly. We don't like it when people lie to us."
- "Avoid yelling. This only makes us angrier and more defensive."
- "Respect us enough to let us come up with our own opinions. We have to learn how not to agree with you, and still have your respect."
- "Help us with our major problems. This doesn't mean we want you to solve them, just help us by listening and caring."
- "Keep talking to us. We like to know the lines of communication are open between us. However, realize that we will not always want to talk at the same time you want to talk. Be patient with us."

Effective listening probably plays the most crucial part in effective communication. I will discuss listening techniques later in this chapter.

Thinking positively about assertiveness proves decisive. Personal thoughts, beliefs, attitudes, and feelings set the foundation for a parent's behavior. Therefore, parents should focus their attention assertively in each new situation. It all starts with their attitudes toward themselves. When parents have negative attitudes about themselves, their behavior will soon follow. Others who interact with them will naturally react to this behavior in negative ways. This can reinforce a negative cycle until the parent changes direction. To reinstate an assertive position—mentally, emotionally, and physically—parents should alert themselves to their own thoughts. They will want to learn what they are doing, and how they are prompting others to act toward them. Their negative self-talk might include:

"I am a failure as a parent."
"My teenager thinks that I am stupid."
"I have no control over what happens in this family."

Sometimes, parents will struggle to reverse the negative behavior by themselves. However, they should not be afraid to ask for help from their friends, their family, and other parents who are able to get them out of their slump. Even their teenagers can help. Such negative parents should work with commitment to change the above statements to more positive ones:

"I am a successful parent."
"My teenager is willing to listen when I talk."
"I can set family goals, and carry them out."

Parents can take positive steps to empower themselves with assertive thoughts. They can start by repeating *positive self-statements* often. This will require them to develop complimentary statements about themselves that they learn, word for word. The more specific these self-descriptions, the more likely will be their success. The parent who created the message must then mentally and orally repeat these affirmations on a regular basis. These statements should help parents build self-confidence. Although this might seem like a foolish activity, it produces positive results. It has done so for me.

One year, I crafted some positive self-assertions and followed them up with visual aids. I located colorful pictures that demonstrated my desires for: A certain earning power by the end of that year, a Lexus (paid-in-full) within twelve months, the publication of my first book (which I had not written yet) within eighteen months, and no visits to the doctor (except for check-ups) for two years. I put these pictures into a photo album and looked at them often to remind myself of my goals. What were the results? I surpassed the dollar-figure I had set for myself. I bought the Lexus within two days of my goal date. My first book was published within the time line I had set. And my health and fitness have reached the highest levels ever.

Assertiveness Involves Good Judgment

Once parents learn assertive behavior, they must use it wisely. Being assertive does not give parents permission to manipulate their children. Nor does skillful assertiveness grant them the right to forget the value of kindness, consideration, empathy, politeness, and more. Especially when it involves their teenagers.

As assertive communicators, parents should be themselves. At the same time, they should respect the feelings and needs of others. When involved in important conversations with their teenagers, parents can exercise assertiveness by not letting telephone calls interrupt these in-person dialogues. Assertiveness does not mean perfection, in parents or in adolescents. However, it does give parents the tools to make worthwhile choices about their direction and achievements. It also gives them skills to handle the consequences of those situations that do not go as they planned. These same skills should also help them counsel their teenagers whenever life does not go as expected, or when the communication process breaks down.

"I am a realist. To me a lot of teens live in fantasy land. Sometimes, I've had to be tough with my message, but I try to tell them the truth about life. Throughout their teens I told them what I tell them now: 'Without an education, you will probably be homeless. Just because you wear good clothes now doesn't mean you will wear them in the future.'"

Eugene, Step-Father
Eric, 20, Social

Parents need to remember that they learn assertiveness. Therefore, they have the ability to change themselves and their direction at any time. It requires hard work and does not come quickly. So, parents, be patient with yourselves. Also, be willing to ask for help when you need it. Even from your teenager.

Problem-Solving: Two-Way Communication

When parents and their teens do turn to each other for help—no matter where the need originated—the situation often involves a problem. HOBY teens said that they primarily seek out their own solutions in efforts to resolve their problems. However, when they do reach out for help, they turn to their parents first.

Step by Step

Problem-solving starts with *mutual respect*. Both parents and their adolescents must enter the process believing in and trusting the other. This acceptance and trust, which must begin long before adolescence, will help parents and their teens exchange ideas, and treat them with the same level of seriousness that they would give their own.

Problem-solving necessitates the *description of the problem*. By describing the problem, the temptation to point fingers and blame others must be excluded. So, parents do not shake their fingers at their teens, and teens do not cross their arms and pull back from their parents. Each party to the problem-solving session focuses on the event or situation. They work together to discover what they need to do to correct it.

"I ask him what the problem is. Then, I tell him what I might do if it were my problem. Then, we talk about ways he would solve the problem."

Ray, Father
Ray Jr., 13, Boy Scouts

Some common problems involve rules of dating, curfew, household responsibilities, scholastic discipline, and money.

"Any family has problems. Some of our problems occur when my kids want to be out past curfew, or they don't get enough sleep because of their busy schedules, or they don't want to help me around the house, or keep their rooms clean. And . . . when they think money grows on trees."

Ginger, Mother
Ginger, 17, Song Leader

"Money, she always wants more money or more things. She will never have everything she needs or wants."

Sandy, Mother
Lisa, 16, Leadership

"Problem? Homework and communication."

Judy, Step-Mother
Amaris, 15, Sports

" . . . Dating boys."

Cindy, Mother
Amie, 16, French Club

"He brings dates to the house and says he has rights, so he should be allowed to have guests in his bedroom. I will allow guys but no girls. Since his teens we have argued about that."

Eugene, Step-Father
Eric, 20, Social

"They sometimes forget their responsibility in helping to maintain cleanliness in the home."

Karen, Mother
Don, 17, Key Club

To find solutions, parents and their teens need to *share information*. Parents will need to respect their teens for their honesty and perspectives. They should avoid accusations, because these will shut down communication efforts more quickly than the melt factor of ice in a microwave on high. By allowing their teens to express ideas honestly, parents underscore their respect for their teens by listening. Every detail can have an impact. When parents share their ideas in the session, they should try to provide new information and outlooks. Although both parents and adolescents need to have the same information about the problem, parents should avoid repeating over and over what the teen already knows.

"Mostly, I listen and sympathize. I also make suggestions, although she perceives them as naive and outdated. I believe all things happen for a reason, and many times I find comfort in merely observing."

Barbara, Mother
Mary, 16, SADD

"I talk to them about my concerns and encourage them to be careful. I say things like 'You might consider. . . ,' 'Some alternatives might be. . . ,' 'What do you think about. . . ?'"

Judy, Step-Mother
Alyse, 13, Music

With all of the information compiled, parents and adolescents need to *craft a workable solution*. To be workable, the solution must be realistic and attainable, with a clear definition of possible *consequences* for incompleteness and *rewards* for completion. It also needs to make sense enough to motivate the teen to pursue it. Both parents and their teens should remember that "passing judgment" on ideas can set back the process. Frequently, ideas offered early in the dialogue that seem insignificant or remote eventually prompt phenomenal solutions.

Parents and teens then need to *take action* on their proposed solution. They need to measure its success, and communicate about how it did or did not work. They should *evaluate* the solution's level of success or failure, and remember this so that they can apply these lessons in similar situations later.

Parents might find themselves walking a fine line with issues and situations involving their teenagers and their teen's friends. When adolescents take on group friendships and identities, they often shed a part of the dependence they have had on their parents. This also affects how and when teens turn to their parents for help with their problems. Knowing that this challenge exists, parents should not forfeit their opportunities to interact with their teens and their teen's groups.

Teenagers' friends reflect their own lives, needs, and choices. When parents shut out these friends, they indirectly shut out their own children. However, when parents include their teens' friends in communications with their own teenagers, they have a much better chance to keep the lines open with their own children. This applies equally well to situations when parents help their adolescents solve problems.

When teens struggle with problems involving their friends, parents should be careful not to draw judgments about the group. Their teen might be having a temporary problem with that group. So the parents' best communication contribution might involve listening only. They should avoid drawing general conclusions, or making hasty decisions, because their teenager will eventually return to that group for friendship and support.

> "I encourage them to take care of their problems on their own. I give advice when asked. After the problem is resolved, I try to talk about how it could be avoided in the future."
>
> *Cindy, Mother*
> *Amie, 16, French Club*

"I try to stay out of it. My child runs it by me. If she asks for advice, I give it. If not, she and her friends work it out. Sometimes, it helps if I tell a story about my own similar troubles as a teenager. It lets her know the same thing happened to me."

Sandy, Mother
Lisa, 16, Leadership

Put Information to Work

Having problems and making mistakes underscores the life of an adolescent. Parents will ease their own burdens when they recognize these influences as normal "teen factors." They will also be better prepared to assist their teens in their own efforts at figuring things out.

Much of the confusion teens experience, and the problems they confront, track back to their own lack of information. Parents need to know that the better informed their teenagers are, the more responsibly they will probably act. Parents have their best chance to succeed when they provide their teens with information that is factual, minus the parental spin. At this stage of information-sharing, parents also need to be careful about adding their own personal propaganda to the lesson. Such insertions can taint the entire message, by giving the impression they are trying to control their children. They should focus primarily on honesty and reality.

Parents can then explain their own values and how these affect the situation. They should be careful not to insist that their teens accept these values as their own. Hopefully, their teens will appreciate how important such values are to their parents, and adopt them when appropriate.

Problem-solving sessions between parents and teen can only succeed, however, if each person involved is committed to the most important communication aspect of all: *Listening*.

Above All Else: Listen

When parents make a commitment to *balanced communication*, they must develop more than the ability to send their messages to their adolescents. Parents need to understand and master receiving messages from their teens. Listening. This skill comprises forty-five percent of the entire communication process, and few of us do it well.

Assertive Listening

Parents must make active commitments to their teenagers in all communications experiences. Parents need to give the process—and their speaking teenager—their full attention: no interruptions. This demonstrates that the parent is an active participant in the conversation, and has respect for the speaking teenager. HOBY teens considered "internal listening"—listening to themselves—the most important kind of listening. However, they placed near-equal emphasis on the need for their parents and their friends to use assertive listening skills with them. Assertive listening requires that the listener:

- *Tune in to the speaker.* This requires the listening parent to stop all other activities that might interfere with the listening process.
- *Attend to the message.* The parent should make eye contact when possible, and give visual feedback, such as nodding and appropriate response gestures.
- *Actively attempt to understand before responding.* The parent needs to think about underlying messages—and feelings—before answering.

Effective listening comprises more than mere *hearing*. It involves hearing, which is only the process by which sound travels from the ears to the brain. Beyond hearing, listening also includes the listener's *understanding* or interpretation of what the speaker said, *evaluation* of that information, and *response* to that which has been heard, understood, and evaluated. Effective listening also involves *feedback*.

Feedback

Feedback comes in various forms. During a dialogue, parents

can give feedback by *paraphrasing* what their teen has said up to that point. Paraphrasing plays a key role in total communication because it reinforces, for the listener and the speaker, that they are both talking about, and responding to, the same information—and their impressions of it. Paraphrasing demonstrates to teenagers that their parents care about what they say and feel. The process itself is easy. Parents simply need to repeat what their teenager says in similar words. They should not interpret or explain, just show their teenager that he or she has been "listened to" and understood. For example, several phrases that will build trust and help ensure that the parent-listener is "on track" with the teenager-speaker include:

- "Are you saying that . . . ?"
- "What I'm hearing you say is. . . ."
- "You have just said that. . . . How do you feel about it?"
- "Since you have told me . . . , what do you plan to do now?"
- "How do you think things will turn out if they go the way you just explained it to me?"
- "Is there anything else you think I should know?"
- "Knowing what you have just told me, is there anything you want me to do?"

Parents need to realize that this is a stage in their teen's life when "solving things for myself" is an important goal. Most adolescents will acknowledge their parents' ability to answer many of their teen problems. However, this does not mean that teens will eagerly relinquish their emerging "right" to find answers for themselves. Knowing this position, parents should recognize that unsolicited information might be unwelcome. So, unless the matter involves a disciplinary or welfare-related matter, parents should make every effort to let their adolescents work out their own problems. This does not preclude, of course, parents from being crucial "partners" in dialogue—as effective listeners.

"My children tell me everything, sometimes more than I want to know. I do my best work as a parent by listening. My motto is: 'If they want my input—they'll ask.' They always do. I'll tell them if I think they're wrong, or tell them when I have faith in their peacemaking skills."

Ginger, Mother
Ginger, 17, Song Leader

"First I just listen. They really need to air it out. Then I express my feelings about the situation, and options on how to handle it. The final decision has to be theirs."

Sandra, Mother
Jasmine, 16, Scholastic

"I listen with respect and trust. I did not feel I had this from my parents. I share my doubts and hopes, and verbalize my decision-making process with her."

Barbara, Mother
Mary, 16, SADD

To encourage feedback, parents should ask relevant, appropriate, and unloaded questions to inspire their teenager's response:
- "How do you feel about this?
- "Do you want to change them? In what ways?"
- "What should we do now that we know more about what happened?"

Feedback should not come across as the parents' effort to control their teenagers. It needs to be genuine, and inspire the teenager to express important personal ideas to parents. Also, parents should avoid bombarding their adolescents with questions. Teens will likely interpret this exchange as an act of war, rather than an effort to demonstrate interest in their needs and personal lives.

When giving feedback to their adolescents, parents should be very careful to avoid mishandling their own responses with such techniques as:

- *Logic.* "What did you expect? To get into the first college you applied to? Life is tougher than that, and you might as well learn it now."
- *Banality.* "There are more fish in the ocean. You can find another college closer to home."
- *Reminiscing,* even *martyrdom.* "When I was your age, I had to work three jobs, and never did get to go to college."
- *Minimizing.* "So what's the big deal? College is college, wherever you go."
- *Blaming.* "You just never seem to know how to make good impressions on other people, even if it's only making an application to college."
- *Self-pity.* "I'm so sorry, son. If I had just worked harder and taken a second job, I could have earned enough to send you to school."
- *Pollyanna-ism.* "Don't worry. Everything always works out for the best."

In addition to giving feedback in problem situations, parents can use *positive feedback* to offer praise. When giving praise, however, parents should avoid sweeping, general statements that praise the teen's "character," rather than the "behavior." For example, parents should not say: "You've always been such a good student, and always will be." This statement sets the teen up for high expectations that, at some point, might be too difficult for the teen to deliver. Nondelivery, in the teen's imagination, will equal failure. A statement such as: "You accomplished a difficult and rewarding task when you built that project for the science fair. Job well done." This sentence of praise addresses the accomplishment—behavior— not the character of the teen who succeeded. The teen will have an easier life, not having to live up to an open-ended standard, especially when parents set them through too-generalized statements of praise.

The Next Step

Parents who put these constructive communication skills to

work with their teenagers will establish opportunities for open two-way interactions—for many parents for the first time. These skills can help them kick off this expanded relationship. The next step will require parents to put the assertive behavior described in this chapter to work, both for themselves and their adolescents.

Quick Points

- Body language—nonverbal communication—comprises fifty-five percent of the communication efforts between parent and child.
- Facial expressions demonstrate how a parent feels. Positive facial expressions, such as the "open face," help communicate a willingness to exchange information.
- Gestures tell what a parent means. Prominent gestures include use of hands and arms.
- Posture demonstrates a parent's level of self-esteem. Posture involves walking, standing, and sitting.
- Use of space defines a parent's ease with sharing territory.
- Eye contact conveys a parent's willingness to connect with his or her adolescent.
- Voice comprises thirty-eight percent of communicated messages. Voice quality includes: pitch, rate, range, volume, rhythm, and more.
- Words account for seven percent of the communication impact. Parents should use the "spoken word" when possible.
- Short words help listeners comprehend meanings more readily than longer ones. This goes for short sentences as well.
- Parents should encourage their teens to use "feeling" words when possible. This helps connect messages at the human level.
- Parents can begin communicating effectively right now by wearing their confidence.
- Humor can add tremendous assistance to communications between parents and teenagers.

- Effective written communications often help parents make positive points with their teenagers.
- Beyond the mere communication of ideas, most parents want to know how to feel positive about what they say and do. This involves *assertive* behavior.
- Assertiveness will help parents promote mutual respect in their relationships with their teens. It also helps them act in their best interests, and in the best interests of their teens.
- Assertive behavior also encourages parents to ask for help when they need it.
- Most parents want to put their assertiveness to work through assertive communication.
- Parents who want to create positive connections with their teenagers need to think affirmatively about their communications.
- Positive self-statements can help parents turn their thoughts into actions.
- Assertive behavior involves good judgment, and considerate applications.
- Problem-solving requires balanced communications between parents and their adolescents.
- Problem-solving involves several steps to succeed:
  - Recognition of mutual respect.
  - Description of the problem.
  - Sharing of information.
  - Crafting of a workable solution.
  - Action and review.

- Adolescence, almost by definition, includes mistakes and problems.
- The better-informed teenagers are, the more responsible they will probably act when addressing their problems.
- *Balanced communication* requires that parents and teens know how to make their points, and respond to each other. Even more crucial, each must understand the importance of listening.
- *Assertive listening* involves the parents' active commit-

ment to their teenager in the communication experience. It requires parents, as listeners, to:

- ⤶ Tune in to their speaking teenager.
- ⤶ Attend to the teen's message.
- ⤶ Actively attempt to understand the message before commenting.
- ⤶ Respond when appropriate, without interrupting.

- *Feedback* involves paraphrasing, asking questions, using the right gestures, and listening.
- When giving feedback, parents should be careful about responding with logic, banality, reminisces, minimizing, blame, self-pity, and excessive optimism.
- Feedback can provide positive results when used for praise. However, parents should remember not to give praise that is too general, or that which addresses the character—not the behavior.
- Parents need to encourage their adolescents to solve their own problems.

11
To the Max

The digital clock on the table in the hallway flashed "1:17 AM"—numbers that would represent at least one week's restriction for Sharon. Late again, and no telephone call home to say why.

"2:32 AM" Sharon's parents wrestle with the fears that any parent might have. What could have happened? What do we do? Whom do we call? Moments, seeming like hours, pass.

"2:57 AM" Tiptoeing like a ballerina who dances silently across a stage, Sharon works her way through the back door, toward her bedroom. Just as her hand reaches the brass knob, the flick of the light in the hallway signals that a confrontation is about to begin.

Both parents and teens identify the issue of "rules" as one of their strongest sticking points during the adolescent years. Parents want their teens to respect the rules of the house, such as curfew. Teens want to stretch the boundaries of their lives, the restrictions imposed upon them. All part of growing up for both parents and their teens.

Setting Limits

Setting limits plays a very important part in childhood development from the earliest years, and must be in place long before the child enters adolescence. Limit-setting takes on profound influence, however, when families strive to survive and surpass adolescence, a time when requirements and limits help define relationships and expectations.

The goal of limit-setting must include a few objectives. These should teach the teen how to: Solve problems, make choices, learn to live with the consequences of choices and, if successful, achieve desired behaviors. When setting limits, parents should remember to focus on the teen's action or behavior, not the person or the character.

Parenting Styles

Setting limits goes even further. *Parenting styles* themselves reflect the ways parents set limits and show understanding.

- *Dictator.* Discourages a teen from "talking back," or even explaining when something has happened. Usually this parent disciplines with contempt.
- *Rigid Guider.* Uses power in a positive manner, listening to the teen's position, then quickly decides whether to challenge. Matter-of-fact approach to discipline. Possesses a certain degree of flexibility.
- *Sympathizer.* Compassionate, and a very strong listener. Thinks about all sides of the issue. First response is sorrow for the child.
- *Empathizer.* Anxious. Overly concerned about the teen's welfare and actually willing to take on the teen's problems. Has difficulty between empathy and control.
- *Changer.* Usually does not have a positive sense of self. Easily manipulated by the teenager.

Why is limit-setting so relevant to the entire parenting experience? Because the home environment is where the child first learns about give and take, self and family, and right and wrong. Children who can feel their parents' compassion and understanding will probably accept their parents' limit-setting.

Growing research indicates parenting style—more than the type of family in which a teen resides—influences a teenager's behavior. The quality of the parent-child relationship plays an equally important part.

Because parents serve as the predominant "older influences" in their lives, teens actually expect their parents to set limits. Teens would not likely accept the same restrictions from their peers, nor from their siblings. HOBY teens indicated that their siblings were the least influential people in their lives; only five percent of the respondents said that their siblings had substantial influence over them. Teens eventually listen to their parents, because they have the wisdom to speak from experience and personal mistakes. However, teens want parents who know how to balance firmness with flexibility. They want caring and involved parents who will help them learn and foster good judgment in their own developing lives.

> "I have a curfew, must get my school work done before I do other things, and get a little bit of sleep here and there."
>
> *Alyssa, 15, Letterman*

> "My parents want to know what I am doing, where I am going, and when I will be home."
>
> *Justin, 14, Rural*

> "My parents expect me to be home by curfew . . . to tell them where I'm going, and to have time for my family, too. They want me to go places that will encourage me to keep my morals safe."
>
> *Kristy, 17, Religious*

> "If I am going out I have to be out of the house by 8:00 PM, or I cannot go. Also, if my friends are going to drink, I need to exercise my judgment about going or not going with them."
>
> *Mayte, 19, Cultural*

Unfortunately, some parents exert their authority out of fear, anger, or frustration, maybe even a desire to wield unnecessary control over their children. These motivations do not inspire trust between parents and their teens. Rather, teens learn about their parents' emotions, not the rationale behind the rules. Often, too, this source of disciplining or rule-setting does not connect the reasons for the rules with the rules themselves. Ultimately, the teenager does not learn how to correlate the rules with responsible behavior because of the parents' intervening emotions.

Authoritative parents know the importance of connecting rules and behaviors. They rationally set distinct standards for their teenagers, and expect responsible behavior from them. These parents make the rules, yet are willing to share dialogues with their teens about the rules: open communications, with an emphasis on give and take. They set standards and demonstrate values. Authoritative parents let their teenagers know what they respect, and what they expect. They are willing to change the rules when it makes sense to do so.

Authoritative parents will invoke sanctions, when necessary. However, when they need to invoke discipline, authoritative parents know not to do so in moments of anger. They recognize the importance of privacy, and timeliness, when disciplining their teens. Also . . . the appropriateness of the discipline, matching it with the improper behavior. These parents recognize the value of consistency, both as it applies to discipline and encouragement.

They set limits that result in teenagers seeking and finding their own identities and self-respect. Sometimes, rules evolve from parents' respect for their teenagers.

> "My parents always encourage me to do the right thing, that is, what my heart tells me to do. They set no restrictions on what I do."
>
> *Michael, 16, Leadership*

> "They want me to have fun but, at the same time, they want me to keep my standards up."
>
> *Cara, 15, Rural*

> "My parents tell me that I know right from wrong. Therefore, I have no rules."
>
> *Africa, 19, Cultural*

Testing the Limits

A natural progression for teens occurs when they work their way into relationships with others in their group. They learn to transfer the ability to give (that their parents have taught them) to their friends. People in their group learn to count on them in times of need. It all starts in the family, where teens learn the basics of human relationships.

Turning to a group also involves "stretching" the limits with the family. As teenagers turn outward for new alliances, they also seek themselves. During this period of exploration, adolescents also find that their newfound identity, and independence, require a distinct separation from their parents. To them, two entities cannot share the same space at the same time. Parents' ideals and rules come into conflict with their own.

So, teens explore the "home rules" and seek ways to extinguish them, or at least, elasticize them. When teens do set out to traverse their parents' limits, they need to have clear definitions of the rules that must stand, without exception. Parents should be careful about interceding in some of the personal decisions teens need to make in their day-to-day "survival" with their friends—their group. For example: When to participate in a particular group function, or whom to ask to the dance, or with whom to share a confidence.

"They want me to be on my best behavior and to act like a good teenager, unlike thousands who get into trouble with gangs, drugs, or violence."

Stephanie, 14, Social

"My parents trust my judgment and know the friends I choose aren't the ones that would do anything rash. As long as my mom knows what I'm doing, and where I am, she feels comfortable if I am with my friends."

Reza, 16, Scholastic

However, parents need to stay firm with their limit-setting

when these rules help guide their teenagers toward behaviors that might involve the law, their teen's health, and their long-term welfare. Parents must determine which limits are "negotiable" and which must be set in concrete.

With the negotiable areas, parents can provide alternatives for their teens, and let their teens make adult choices. By setting appropriate limits, parents can still "protect" their teens, yet give them the room to test the limits, and grow into mature decision-makers. This allows teenagers to continue their exploration process. They just need to explore within the parameters set by their parents—people who have already been there and know the consequences.

" . . . By letting her fly now in whatever direction her interests take her, by teaching her to finish what she starts, by making her take responsibility for her actions. To rescue her is to smother her."

Ginger, Mother
Amy, 16, Religious

"I give my teen privacy and space. I don't question everything she does. I give her the chance to grow with fewer limits."

Sandy, Mother
Lisa, 16, Leadership

"I provide basic needs and prepare my teens for entry into the real world. I want to help bridge the gap. I am open and honest about what goes on in the real world—the bad along with the good. I also try to initiate conversations on important life topics, and steer conversations toward building resolutions to cope with future problems."

Steven, Father
Kansa, 17, Scholastic

Making Sense of Rules

Rules help both parents and their teenagers understand how to move forward with their lives. By setting rules for children during early childhood, and living by them, families will learn what to expect from each other. For teens, experiencing their lives with rules will also help them understand what they can expect from their group identities. They learn how to adapt what they learn in their families to their new "families" outside the home.

Expanding Safety Zones

Rules should not be designed to pit parents against teens. Rules should not give adolescents the impression that these rules have been created solely to cause them trouble and frustration. At the same time, parents should remind themselves often that certain rules are crucial to the safety and well-being of their teens, no matter how loud the protests.

Parents also need to remember, that their teens are living by rules established by others as well. Teachers and administrators will set up guidelines for school attendance and mandated behavior on school grounds. Employers will define work rules and expectations. Peer groups will determine their own friendship rules and regulations. And then there's the rest of the world.

Even by recognizing that these many sets of rules influence their teenagers, parents can put "perspective" to work. Understanding serves well here. Teens need to know that their parents recognize that the pressures on their lives come from many directions. In return, parents need to identify and clarify why their teenagers must accept, as certain high-level priorities, the nonnegotiable rules they set. Parents need to have faith in their adolescents to know how to prioritize the rules in their lives. These same teenagers will probably struggle to understand which rules supersede others, but this stimulates a viable part of the growth-and-choice aspect of their lives.

> "Family responsibilities, school work, church responsibilities are not to be neglected. They know they must balance time and activities."
>
> *Karen, Mother*
> *Don, 17, Key Club*

"I expect my kids to be honest and respectful of others. I want them to follow a few basic rules we have in the house, and strive to achieve a happy life."

Steven, Father
Amaris, 15, Sports

"I hope for creative and healthy activities in safe environments, and expect them to take their good sense and judgment with them. They know their curfew; they know not to get isolated from the crowd. They know not to indulge in drugs, sex, and alcohol."

Sandra, Mother
Amber, 14, Social

Parents have a perfect opportunity to help their teenagers in another way, too. They can help their teens understand the distinct ways in which following rules can lead to rewards. By following the rules, teenagers can learn to master new tasks, skills, ideas, or practices. Once they learn to master these newfound abilities, parents should encourage their teenagers to take an active role in creating and implementing new rules. Parents and teens will benefit from working together to develop these next-level house rules.

Parents and teens should focus their attention on a few workable guidelines for these rules.

- *Rules should be designed in positive ways.* They should keep the best interests of the most people in mind. This will start with meeting basic needs that focus on physical and emotional considerations.
- *Parents need to encourage their teens to grow responsibly with their rules.* To reach self-empowerment, teens need to take care of themselves physically, mentally, emotionally, and spiritually. Adolescents need to learn how to take care of their own needs first, before they can help their friends and their group. "Needs" are those parts of their lives that they cannot exist without for even a short time. First things first.

Teens must understand that to take care of themselves, they must eat well, strive for fitness, and avoid abuses that can injure them and others. They must also stay alert, as their empowerment will require a strong dose of commitment and positive direction. As teens profit from their own empowerment and expansion of skills and responsibilities, others—especially their parents and their group—will also benefit.

- *Testing rules will expose teenagers to new consequences.* As they expand their roles in rule-setting, teenagers will also learn about new outcomes for expected behaviors. In addition, they will expose themselves to new consequences for mishandled behaviors.
- *When teenagers take risks, they learn to appreciate the value of rules.* Understanding why certain rules are required, adolescents will learn the values of these dictates. When experimenting beyond known rules can reap better rules, both parents and teens should collaborate on new rules. Together, parents and teens should always remember the benefits, as well as the potential consequences, when crafting new rules.

Quick Points

- *Parents must set limits* for their teenagers to ensure the survival of the family during that child's adolescence.
- Limit-setting should teach teens how to: Solve problems, make choices, learn to live with the consequences of their choices, and achieve desired behaviors.
- *Parenting styles* reflect the ways parents set limits. Styles include: the *dictator,* the *rigid guider*, the *sympathizer,* the *empathizer,* and the *changer.*
- Parenting style serves as one of the strongest influences affecting teenage behavior.
- Most teenagers actually expect their parents to set rules for them, and are relieved when they do.
- Some parents exert their authority in anger, frustration, or fear.

- Parents need to set standards rationally for their teenagers, and expect responsible behavior from them.
- Authoritative parents practice open communications with their teens, and are flexible with their rule-setting.
- When authoritative parents invoke sanctions, they recognize that to apply sanctions requires good judgment and application.
- Teens learn to transfer their knowledge of limits to their group affiliations.
- Teens will explore their "home rules" and seek ways to extinguish them, or at least elasticize them, when they interact with their friends in the group.
- Parents need to stay firm with their limit-setting with rules that help guide their adolescents in areas involving the law, their teen's health, and long-term welfare. These rules are nonnegotiable.
- Rules help parents and their adolescents learn how to move forward with their lives.
- Rules should not be designed to pit parents against their teenagers.
- Parents need to recognize that their children also live by rules established by others: Teachers and administrators, employers, peer groups, and so on.
- Parents can help their teenagers learn the advantages of following the rules.
- Guidelines for following rules should help teens learn that:
    - Rules should be designed in positive ways.
    - Parents need to encourage their teens to grow responsibly with family rules.
    - Testing rules will expose teenagers to new consequences.
    - When teenagers take risks, they learn to appreciate the value of rules.

12
Teaching By Example

Parents' Day at Evermore High School—each year about this time, fathers and mothers attend their teens' classes throughout the day. They describe their jobs, careers, volunteerism, or whatever they chose to do with their lives. Warren had been dreading this day. His father was scheduled for second period. Soon it would be over, he hoped, knowing that he couldn't remember a longer sixty minutes in the entire year. Some fathers made a lot of money. Others had positions of power and respect, making a difference in the community. Still others focused their time and energies on their families. Warren had nothing to look forward to; his father did none of these.

When teenagers start to look within their own families for answers about adulthood, they primarily turn to their parents for direction. These information-hungry teens seek parental assistance in posturing themselves for their own futures—parents to show them, by example, what to expect of themselves and others in adulthood. Or, at least they try to find an affirmative representation of what they, as teenagers, should seek for themselves in the postadolescent years.

With Eyes to the Parents

Today's teenagers face a dilemma with their parents. They are seeking direction and guidance from their parents, to "sample by example" the next tier of their development—adulthood. At the same time, their parents are actually going through their own transitional stage. Although most parents have moved well beyond their own adolescence, at least in calendar years, many of them still "fall back" to their own adolescence, emotionally and psychologically. They might mentally return to these years because of pleasurable memories; or because life seemed more simplistic; or because someone else—their parents—hovered over them, taking full responsibility.

With these parental returns to adolescence also come the matching behaviors, not all of which are positive. Some parents avoid adult obligations: paying the bills, going to work, or honoring their commitments. Some participate in illegal activities: drugs, drinking and driving, or violent behavior. Some ignore parental responsibilities: establishing important family rules, communicating with their teens, or knowing their adolescent's friends.

Unfortunately, when parents avoid their adult roles, they often pass on these avoidance attitudes and behaviors to their teenagers. Why? Because parents serve as the most potent role models for their own teenagers, whether the behavior is positive or negative. So when parents "do their own thing," their teens will likely "do their own thing," too. Often, parental and adolescent behaviors actually parallel each other.

With the decision to become parents, adults must recognize the responsibility to commit their best efforts to the child-raising *process*. Beyond the basics of taking care of primary physical and economic needs, this process also includes:

- Understanding of, and contribution to, the natural developmental phases that their children undergo. This means parents need to help their children master the stages of their lives, from childhood to adolescence and into adulthood.
- Support and respect *for* their children, in exchange for respect and loyalty *from* their children.
- Setting rules for, and granting freedoms to, their teens. These rules must relate to their teens' demonstrations of responsible behavior.

- Providing, by example, appropriate behaviors and attitudes from which their teenagers can make choices about their own lives. This includes everything from following rules to setting goals to selecting friends.

Setting Examples

One important way for parents to succeed as role models involves setting standards. Teenagers will only be inclined to apply their parents' standards to their own lives when they understand the reasons behind them. When they perceive *why* their parents think what they think, say what they say, and do what they do. Teenagers seek purpose, and they look to their parents for it.

> "Role modeling is the single most important issue. I show my children responsibility and self-respect. I do not go out drinking all night, or get involved in short-term affairs, one after the other. I do not take drugs or smoke. Hopefully, some day, this will have some meaning for them."
>
> *Sandra, Mother*
> *Amber, 14, Social*

> "Actions speak louder than words. Role modeling is very important. Parents need always to be aware that their children are watching them."
>
> *Karen, Mother*
> *Don, 17, Key Club*

> "I think role modeling is the most important thing in the child's development. When they are small, the parent is who they see. It is a big responsibility to be a parent. I have taught the children that they are very fortunate to have what they have. I feel the home life will reflect the outcome of who they will become."
>
> *Sandy, Mother*
> *Lisa, 16, Leadership*

"Kids do what they see being done, not what we tell them to do. I try to be a positive example of a good friend, wife, and mother."

Cindy, Mother
Amie, 16, French Club

When parents want to make a point with their actions, they should express in words the "why" of their behavior. For example, after writing a check out to a local nonprofit, parents can tell their teenager: "We feel good about sharing our good fortune with children in the community who need help."

In reverse, words alone will fall short if not supported by actions. Telling their teenagers that it is important to be unselfish means little, if anything, when parents do not demonstrate what they say. Maybe they could volunteer several hours a month to help handicapped toddlers in a local rehabilitation facility. Put simply, because we tend to be a visual society—we need to see to believe—it is vital that parents do what they say. This criterion serves as a bare minimum for positive role modeling.

Parents can take another step forward by encouraging their teens to take responsibility. Of course, this requires parents to act responsibly in the same ways they expect their teenagers to behave. Parents cannot come home intoxicated, toss their keys on the counter, and stagger to bed, and the next evening tell their eighteen-year-old son, "We know that you will not drink before leaving the party."

A third way parents can demonstrate positive role modeling involves how they handle their own problems and challenges. By showing their children, by example, effective ways to solve problems or answer questions, parents will empower their teens to do the same. For example, when parents work out the family budget and include their teens in the process of balancing income with outflow . . . teens will learn the importance in spending their own money wisely. Teenagers generally do not have superhuman powers to learn by unconscious osmosis. They need help.

"Parents must provide a good example. I do not give my children unrealistic expectations."

Karen, Mother
Don, 17, Key Club

"My son learns by watching me. One way I set an example is the way I act with my own adult friends."

Ray, Father
Ray Jr., 13, Boy Scouts

Working parents have special opportunities to provide positive role modeling examples. Not necessarily will the teens become clones of their own parents. They do, however, learn about the workplace, the work ethic, their parents' involvement in relationships outside the home, the exchange of respect between people at different levels of the employment tier, and much more. Parents can accomplish a great deal by taking their teens to work with them, to expose their children to the people who are outside the home.

Sharing Values

The list would run pages. The meanings would differ from parent to parent, child to child. The underscoring question of the exercise: Which *values* make sense today?

Experts on every continent could define and describe what values rise to the top in their various cultures. The teenagers in Part 1 stated the primary importance of trust, loyalty, and commitment in their friendships. Parents would undoubtedly agree with these values. With these, and all of the hundreds of other important "value areas," parents have a fundamental responsibility. They must set examples, as positive role models, for the virtues they want their teens to adopt. Attitudes, words, behaviors. Consistency also counts for a lot. Parents need to demonstrate regularly and often the values that reflect their positive actions and reactions to people and events around them. Here is a small sample of virtues parents will probably want to encourage in their teens.

Courage. Working together during a family crisis. Turning to each other with support, and for support. Lending strengths to others.

Honesty. Returning the right amount of money for purchases to a supermarket checker when the receipt is short. Admitting mistakes. Crying when something sad or sentimental happens.

Responsibility. Arranging a work schedule to be home when the kids return from school. Making ends meet. Knowing how and when to ask for help, and when to count on self.

Love. Giving hugs and gentle pats on the back. Sacrifice. Unconditional support and tolerance.

Unselfishness. Praising teenagers for their contributions to family projects. Sharing personal possessions with others. Splitting fun money four ways instead of three.

Hope. Overcoming temporary and permanent disabilities to excel in activities. Knowing that "fresh starts" begin right now. Believing that "first steps" can take us miles.

Independence. Learning how to enjoy private time as much as group time. Thinking and acting individually, detached from group pressure. Knowing when to handle situations alone, and when to ask for help.

Self-discipline. Saying "no" when others feel pressured to say "yes." Giving up one thing for something more important. Putting fitness and mental well-being ahead of unhealthy indulgences.

Kindness. Being available to a needy friend. Giving assistance when a teen gives a pleading look. Smiling when it would be easier to scowl.

Fairness. Encouraging everyone to give input before coming to a conclusion. Reading the newspaper and asking "Why?" or "What's missing?" when the story is incomplete or biased. Listening, listening, listening.

Patience

Patience would probably score high as a value with parents. Being patient might include refusing to let other people flaunt their own definitions and applications of "good parenting." These outsiders might be parents' parents, parents' children, other relatives, neighbors, teachers, or the community-at-large. Parents should remember that their successes with positive parenting and role modeling will derive directly from what they believe and how they deliver it. Of course, ultimate success will require positive attitudes and actions, which will influence others, too.

> "I believe in being a positive role model. I am good to myself, good to my children, and good to my friends. I encourage strong qualities in us all. I hope seeing this, talking about it, and doing it will help them use good judgment in their lives."
>
> *Sandra, Mother*
> *Jasmine, 16, Scholastic*

Patience also helps parents accept that they are imperfect. Positive role modeling empowers parents to recognize that all of their efforts will not succeed, and all of their wise counsel might not work. Because they are imperfect, however, patient parents recognize the value of the *search* for answers and directions. This search often translates into the most important demonstration of positive role modeling for their adolescents.

When Teens Turn to Friends

When teenagers do not find the role models they seek in their own *families of origin*, they will naturally turn elsewhere. One popular alternative: *families of choice*. These might include friends and their families, teachers, other adults. Often, teens turn solely to their friends. They seek role models who can assist them in their transitions from adolescence into adulthood. People who stand ahead of them, to give them options for "who I want to be." Unfortunately, their friends and their peer groups usually reflect the same level of development. Therefore, this will probably limit the extent to which this role modeling can influence teens about their "future" development. However, this phenomenon should not discount the value of friendship in the role modeling process.

When teens do turn to their friends for role modeling, the group can offer support and kinship to the teen seeking direction. This friendship link can actually surpass that of the genetic links. Choice underscores the reason. Teens who define themselves, at least in part, by the friends they select, will turn to these friends when they need answers. Even when the answers might not be complete, or even on target. At least, the group can provide a foundation from which to search beyond, or a base of operation to which they can return from their periodic searches. After all, the rest of the group is probably going through a parallel experience: The pursuit of positive role models.

Action Steps

Parents do not need to set aside a day on the calendar to begin role modeling for their children. In fact, if parents wait until their children reach adolescence, they have waited too long. They must start the "life-by-example" teaching method when their children are toddlers, or younger. However, not all parents want to take on this responsibility at any stage of their children's lives.

Outside Role Models

One role-modeling choice parents can exercise involves passing these tasks on to another adult. This decision produces *passive role modeling*, and often occurs when parents encourage teenagers to seek nonparental *outside role models*. These outsiders provide external influence and lifestyle choices to the teenager. This role modeling becomes passive when these other adults do not interact directly with the teenager. For example, high-profile leaders or national activists. More involved outside role models might be the parents of an adolescent friend. These particular role models can serve active or passive parts in the teenager's life.

As mentioned in the previous section, many adolescents seek outside role models in their own groups. Because some parents have difficulty in serving as primary role models for their own children, outside role models take over. Teens need someone to fill this void. A living example.

> "If my children couldn't look to us, their parents, as role models, I would want them to model themselves after honest, hard working, and honorable men or women wherever they find them in life. I also hope they always turn to their faith for spiritual role models."
>
> *Ginger, Mother*
> *Amy, 16, Religious*

> "I wouldn't select role models for my kids, even when they were teens, because everyone is a human being. When role models fall, the kids might take it hard. My motto is: Be your own role model."
>
> *Eugene, Step-Father*
> *Eric, 20, Social*

> "The best role models are strong adults who have had problems, yet came out on top. And they became better because of their problems. Not movie stars, sports figures, models, and so on."
>
> *Cindy, Mother*
> *Amie, 16, French Club*

> "Actually, some of the parents portrayed on TV handle real-world problems well: Financial troubles, death, or whatever."
>
> *Ray, Father*
> *Ray Jr., 13, Boy Scouts*

Family Meetings, Family Traditions

For parents who want to take a more active part in the role modeling responsibilities with their teenagers, many options exist. One choice is *family meetings*, where everyone gathers regularly to discuss family needs, concerns, possible resolutions, and more. During this shared time, everyone respects everyone, and parents encourage open communication. Unfortunately, according to HOBY participants, fifty-four percent of them either do not have shared family time, or have it only when their parents decide to schedule it.

Family traditions comprise another important ingredient to positive role modeling. Parents can establish and reinforce family traditions, because these help create and perpetuate family bonds. They empower parents, and their children, to experience and pass on family sensitivity through the celebration of special events. Birthdays, anniversaries, special occasions, family successes, and more.

> "My children have a strong sense of family, both past and present. We talk about traditions and deceased family members. We do a lot of family activities in our family and extended family. I have influenced my kids to pick friends with the same values."
>
> *Cindy, Mother*
> *Amie, 16, French Club*

> "My mother doesn't mind how much time I spend with friends. However, my father insists that going out every two weeks with a friend is enough, and you should spend almost every waking moment with family."
>
> *LiAn, 16, Scholastic*

Shared Time

Shared time also helps parents demonstrate positive imaging with their teenagers. Family meetings involve family issues and needs. Shared time involves "being together" for something special, or nothing special at all. It involves parents and their teens, sharing experiences, ideas, memories, words, and so on. Togetherness, in terms of *quality time* and *quantity of time*.

Parents need to realize that they cannot mete out time in small doses and hope that their teenagers will settle for less. Positive parenting requires that adolescents have prioritized time and space in their parents' lives, not just allotments slipped in between work and other professional or personal agenda items. This requires that parents be willing to take control away from the electronic baby sitters that often otherwise supervise their children—television, radio, CD, video games. They need to have one-to-one time, eye-to-eye contact, and total communication experiences with their children. This does not require parents to spend money, just time.

Even when teenagers fervently seek their own independence and self-identity, most of them still hunger for shared time with their parents. Parents generally demonstrate responsibility in their investments of time, money, and energy. Yet, they will experience no greater, farther-reaching returns than the platinum dividends they will enjoy when they share time in building relationships with their own teenagers. Through this union, teenagers can know their parents, and appreciate them as positive role models in their lives. What a legacy!

Quick Points

- When teenagers start to look within their own families for answers about adulthood, they primarily turn to their parents for direction.
- Some parents have difficulty facing their teenagers' growing-up needs, because these parents have reverted to their own adolescence, emotionally and psychologically.
- When parents avoid their own adult roles, they are likely to pass along these avoidance attitudes and behaviors to their teens.
- When parents make a commitment to the *parenting process*, they should pledge themselves to:
  - Understand and contribute to the natural developmental phases their children will experience.

- Support and respect their teenagers.
- Set rules for, and grant freedoms to, their adolescents.
- Provide, by example, appropriate behaviors and attitudes: positive role modeling.

- One important mandate for role modeling involves establishing standards.
- When parents want to make a point with their actions, they should explain why that action is important. In turn, when they say something is important, they need to support their words with actions.
- Parents should encourage their teenagers to take responsibility. They can demonstrate accountability through their own behavior.
- Parents also show positive role modeling in the ways they handle their own problems and challenges.
- Working parents have special opportunities to provide positive role modeling for their teenagers.
- Parents have a fundamental responsibility to establish basic values for their teenagers to follow. For example: *Courage, honesty, responsibility, love, unselfishness, hope, independence, self-discipline, kindness,* and *fairness.*
- Parents will also appreciate the virtue of *patience,* both in themselves and in their teenagers.
- Teens often turn to their group when they do not find appropriate role models in their own homes. However, their friends are generally experiencing the same level of search. This might limit how much teens can pattern themselves after their friends when looking to their own "future" development.
- Some parents relinquish their role-modeling responsibilities and encourage their adolescents to look elsewhere, to outsiders: nonparental role models.
- Parents can take positive action steps to create role modeling opportunities for themselves through:
  - Family meetings.
  - Family traditions,.
  - Shared time: quality and quantity.

13
Fostering Friendship
Parents and Teens

Everyone around her, including her parents, relatives, and anyone else who knew her would describe Monica as a loner. She had few friends in her life, and did not belong to groups. Yes, a loner. Monica rarely indulged in conversations of more than three minutes with her parents. Even these were limited to yes-no responses. Through the years, Monica's parents adjusted to Monica's "style" but realized that soon she would experience a life-changing experience: Graduation. With it, life would shove a whole new set of rules and expectations at Monica. They just knew that their "little girl" wasn't ready. Not yet.

In chapter 1 of this book, I explained how parents and other societal influences furnish today's teenagers with tickets on the "jet track," and thrust them through their adolescent years. Parents have many expectations, one being that their teenagers enjoy immediate popularity, and forever be surrounded by hordes of friends. And, of course, their adolescents will thrive on this constant attention. Not necessarily so.

Everyone Wants to Be Popular, Right?

Popularity, and all that goes with it—recognition, acceptance, approval—signal something very important for teenagers. It represents a marker that they have "passed a test" for inclusion in the group—someone, or many someones, like them. That's terrific. At least, parents might presume so.

A teen's "popularity ratings" often justify all the years of support parents have rendered up to this crucial time in their teen's life. Popularity has become synonymous with, and fundamental to, likability, achievement, and ultimate success. For many parents, a peer group's acceptance of their child can be equalled only by the first landing on the moon, the discovery of penicillin, or the creation of interactive computer learning programs.

Prior to the adolescent years, discerning whether a child is popular can be difficult. In preadolescence, children have playmates, anyone who will share their toys with them and vice-versa. Companionship comes easily.

During their teenage years, however, adolescents have expanded needs, the first of which is to figure out just who they are. Seeking individual identities takes a lot of their time. While teens strive to figure out who they are, they are also trying to select their friends and the groups they want to join. Simultaneously, these potential friends are also checking them out. How well this two-way "selection process" works often determines the first experience of adolescent acceptance and popularity, or rejection.

"I hang around with different people at different times. I spend most of my time, however, with one girl because we are so alike."

Cara, 15, Rural

"I don't look at popularity! I do have a lot of friends, but I keep to myself. I just hang out with people I've known for a long time."

Erika, 18, Employment

"More people like me than don't like me. I try not to be mean or unkind to anyone in any group. I spend most of my time with my close friends, the ones I've known for the longest time."

Reza, 16, Scholastic

"I can blend with any group I've ever needed to, but I've never completely belonged to one group."

Chris, 17, Wrestler

"Some people think I'm a nerd because of my religion. They don't think I'm cool, because I follow my church standards well."

Michael, 16, Religious

Popularity: Not a Universal

Teens might experience a reduced sense of self-esteem if they do not pass their first popularity test. Or they might feel good enough inside, certain about their self-worth, that the initial rejection does not affect them.

Teenagers might not make friends or join groups easily, because of changes in their lives. When they were younger children, life was basic and made few demands on playmates. However, with entrance into adolescence, interests change. Teenagers look at friends in new and different ways. For teenagers, the process of finding out where they belong and who wants to include them is not easy.

Popularity often pivots around appearance in the teen years. However, this criterion does not always indicate true friendship. Groups that include teenagers because of what they have in common generally do not require movie-star good looks as a membership qualification. *Real friendships*, not just popularity, will significantly influence how teenagers shape their adolescent years. When teenagers actually find a circle of friends—groups—that share their interests, and accept them for who they are, teenagers more easily move toward positive definitions of themselves.

Parents need to recognize that *peer bonding* does not develop instantly, and often produces its own ups and downs. When teenagers do not readily fit into a particular group, some parents take this personally. Minimally, they might experience concern for their child. Some parents might go so far as to assert themselves to correct this social and emotional situation. Others prefer to get involved by giving a little direction.

> "I never select their friends but I try to guide or 'warn' them if I see something to worry about. I know they will have to make the ultimate friendship decision on their own."
>
> *Sandra, Mother*
> *Amber, 14, Social*

> "I do not try to influence whom my kids associate with. I do try to teach my kids what attributes good friends should possess. I allow my kids to make mistakes concerning the trials of friendship, so they can learn firsthand about true friendship. I tell them friends should respect them for who they are and what they believe."
>
> *Steven, Father*
> *Ari, 19, Social*

> "I don't pick my children's friends. I do teach them what kind of a person to be, and give them the freedom to think for themselves. I'm usually the one who says 'Don't forget to invite so and so. She needs friends, too.'"
>
> *Ginger, Mother*
> *Amy, 16, Religious*

Still other parents lose patience with their teenagers. This rejection, in some parents' eyes, reflects on them. "What's wrong with my child? I was always popular." Some of this lost patience also camouflages the bruised expectations parents might have for their children. These parents might feel disappointment when their children do not fulfill their own vicarious hopes for popularity. When the bonding does not "stick" on the first try, however, there might be several reasons why.

Maybe the teenager is not ready, for whatever reason, to join a peer group. Some teenagers do not know yet what they like, or they might be shy, or they might feel uncomfortable with older kids. To help with this integration process, teenagers need to find the right group. This takes time, as determined by the teenager's clock, not the parents'.

Because teenagers need to join the right groups when they are ready, parents sometimes get impatient. This can pressure teenagers to join groups prematurely, sometimes forcing them to join inappropriate groups. Just because their parents think they should belong to a particular group does not mean that this group provides the best friendship circle for the teenager.

Also, some parents have a preconceived notion about how many friends or groups their teenagers should have in their lives. In reality, every adolescent is distinctive, with special needs and affinities. No formulas, no magic tricks, no computer programs exist that can predetermine and deliver how many friends each teenager will have.

> "I've been very lucky. I haven't had to exert influence over how she chooses her friends. She tends to pick friends who are mature and have the same values she has. My child has good judgment about who she picks, and how many."
>
> *Sandy, Mother*
> *Lisa, 16, Leadership*

Many teenagers deal with the pressure of popularity by selecting an *exclusive* or *best friend*. By just having to be responsible to one person, as well as only having to count on one person, teenagers "save themselves" from the pressures of socializing with many people.

Ninety-eight percent of HOBY respondents believe they can inexplicably trust their "best friends." For some teenagers, group membership creates stress that they struggle to survive—just too many people when they are not ready for multiple friendships and group experiences. Also, by having only one friend, some teenagers feel "safe," because this is manageable. It often ties them to the preadolescent years when life was simpler, and expectations were fewer.

Even loners—teens who have no friends—use their adolescence as a testing period. Often, they strategically seek which group or groups to join, and which people to call friends. For many loners, the process presents greater challenges, because they do not have singular friends to help them bridge the gap between early childhood and adolescence. However, this will not necessarily cripple them, as many teenagers make the transition quite successfully.

Whatever the friendship choices, parents need to understand and appreciate that their teenagers have their own styles in friendship-building, and the rate at which they grow their own friendships. Tolerance and respect for this process will help parents make the adjustment to their teen's friendship evolution. Also, when parents help unload external burdens and expectations from their children's shoulders, these teenagers will likely survive and surpass the traumas that partner with the adolescent period of life.

Taking Steps

As much as they might wish and hope and cross their fingers, parents do not have the ability to make friends for their teenagers. However, parents can help their adolescents who might be having difficulty making friends. They can start by exploring the reasons for the struggle.

By their very nature, teenagers struggle daily with their own identities. They can be moody, irresponsible, grouchy, quick-tempered, sarcastic, and dozens of other mood-oriented dispositions, sometimes all at once. Knowing that these mood swings help define adolescence, parents should give their teenagers a little room to stretch their emerging personalities. However, sometimes parents really do not like these behaviors, and prefer not to spend time around their children.

Rather than giving teenagers the distinct impression they do not like them, parents need to talk with their children. Parents need to describe candidly the behaviors they want their teens to change, and why. Again, they should remember to discuss the behavior, not to attack the teenager as a person. Behavior is the issue, not character or personhood. By going too far with commentary, parents can wreak irreversible damage on their teenager; surely this is not their intent.

Parents can accomplish part of this task by not conjuring up unreachable notions of "what my teenager should be"—computer genius, sports superstar, financial magnate. They should not let preconceived expectations of their teenager color the real-world experiences with their adolescent's development—with all of its successes and near-successes.

When teens have difficulty making friends, parents should find reasons to praise, not criticize, their teenagers. Obviously, most teenagers already know the disappointment of rejection; they do not need a second layer from their parents. Besides, just because some teenagers do not have friends "on schedule" does not mean that they will never have friends. Parents need to remember that each teenager has a different developmental clock, and this includes socialization with others.

Parents should also take time to get to know and appreciate the few friends that their teenagers might have. Friendship choices belong to the people who make them. So when parents chide their children for the friends they do select, they are also challenging their own children. Friends, especially in early experiences of friendship, mirror the teenagers who select them.

Lead, Don't Push

Another extreme behavior parents should avoid involves "pushing." Parents should feel comfortable with the role modeling tips I explained in chapter 12. These will help them understand how to "show" their teenagers about successful relationships.

Parents should avoid aggressive parenthood. They should not shove their teenagers into social situations that force their children to make friends or join groups. When teenagers are ready to make friends, they will do so. Forced friendships, especially when the parents are the enforcers, can actually poison teenagers about particular groups. "If that's what my parents want, it's not for me."

Parental interference, therefore, can actually preclude a teenager's involvement with a particular group. Ironically, if given the opportunity, the teenager might have enjoyed involvement with that particular group. Not, however, when the parent pushes, rather than leads, the way. In fact, this kind of interference often prompts teenagers to look in opposite directions for group identities. "I'll show them" might fortify the teenager's search for self and friends.

Unfortunately, these retreats to unlikely or inappropriate groups can cause difficulty for the newly recruited teenagers and their parents. Some of these groups, especially antisocial ones, might disregard laws, use drugs, abuse people, trash neighborhoods, and more.

> "My parents hate my friends. My dad says he doesn't trust them, and thinks they're all dope addicts."
>
> *Jason, 17, Gang*

When teenagers join these types of negative groups, parents will need to take action. Merely standing by when teenagers participate in destructive antisocial activities can cause permanent effects. And the teenager might be too immature to understand these negative influences until it is too late. Social rejection, dropping out of school, criminal records, and other damage often serve as the byproducts of membership in antisocial groups.

The extent of parental involvement in their teenager's friendship building will vary. The contributions they make and the direction they offer will provide lasting influences throughout their child's adolescence. From the primary vantage points I have discussed throughout this chapter, parents have opportunities to make a positive difference. They can provide crucial input to their teenager's friendship development, from inception to fruition. However, there's more.

Pacing and Perspective:
On to the Positive

As teenagers move into their groups, assisted gently by their parents, these same adolescents might choose to shed their families in the process. For some reason, teens often find it easier to separate completely from their original nurturers to ensure a proper place for those who replace them—their friends.

The parents' agenda might indicate space for both the family and the group. Parents should recognize the importance of balance between family and friends. Teenagers look at it differently: It's one or the other. For now, "the other"—friends and the group—holds a special allure. Newness, freshness, the unknown. A first step into new adventures. No history to bog them down.

An interesting aspect of mutuality adds a spin to the separation process. Just as the teenagers are pulling away from their parents, these same parents are experiencing a separation from their teenagers. In fact, separation affects the entire family. Some parents have great difficulty with their teenagers' efforts to separate. They tend to want to reign in their teenagers, or hover over them. Other parents deal with separation by distancing themselves from their adolescents. This helps them avoid the eventual pain that the "loss of the child" creates.

In the healthiest of situations, the transition between dependency on parents and individuality will produce a new relationship between parents and their teenagers. The result: balance. Both parents and their teenagers will learn to balance between their needs to be attached to each other and their needs to have separate lives.

Letting Go

When parents learn to let go of their teenagers, they do more than just release their children into the bigger world. They encourage them to develop self-reliance and to take risks. This helps their teenagers learn about the world outside their front door. It helps them discover how they fit into the larger scheme of things, starting with their groups.

By letting go, parents also give permission to their teens to make mistakes, even fail. Parents realize that they must stop rescuing their children. After all, mistakes provide crucial opportunities for learning about what works and what doesn't.

This signals the time for teenagers to plot their own destinies and draw their own maps. They might take some wrong turns. But parents should have faith in their teenagers. They should believe that their traveling offspring will find their ways, and most likely succeed in their journeys. Often, too, when these travelers discover new territories, they will learn to appreciate their homes of past. For most teenagers, subsequent journeys will include those that take them home, back to their parents and their families, full circle.

Quick Points

- Popularity, and all that goes with it—recognition, acceptance, approval—signal something very important for teenagers.
- Prior to adolescence, determining whether children are popular is difficult. Preadolescents focus on playmates, rather than popularity.
- During adolescence, teenagers have expanded needs, the first of which is to figure out who they are.
- Popularity does not serve as a universal standard for emergence into adulthood. Teenagers might not easily make friends or join groups, because of changes in their lives.
- Adolescent popularity often pivots around physical appearance. However, this criterion does not always reflect true friendship.
- *Peer bonding* does not occur instantly, and usually involves ups and downs.
- Parents sometimes get impatient with their teenagers' lack of friends or group memberships. This can pressure teens to join groups prematurely.

- Many teenagers deal with the pressures of popularity by selecting just one *best friend*.
- Even "loners"—teenagers who have no friends—use their adolescence as a testing period.
- Whatever their friendship choices, teenagers have their own styles of friendship building.
- Parents do not have the skill, or the right, to make friends for their teenagers.
- Parents should avoid devising unattainable friendship goals and expectations for their teenagers.
- When teenagers have difficulty making friends, their parents should find reasons to praise, not criticize, their teenagers.
- Parents should avoid pushing their teenagers into groups. This results in *aggressive parenthood*.
- Forcing friends on teenagers can actually poison these adolescents about friendship.
- Parental interferences can preclude a teenager's involvement with a particular group and, in contrast, drive that teenager to join an inappropriate group.
- As teenagers find their place in the groups of choice, they often shed their families.
- The separation of teens from their parents can spawn a reciprocal separation of parents from their teens.
- When parents let go of their teens, this release often inspires a freedom—a freedom for the teenager to return home when ready.

Afterword
An Open Dialogue

Thirteen chapters, now what? That was my question when I got to this part of the book, but I knew something else needed to be said. When I pondered just what, I "listened" once again to the hundreds of people who had direct input in this book. I had asked them all: "If you were to write this book, what else would you want to say?" They told me. I thought you, the reader, would be interested in the thoughts and needs that both teenagers and parents wanted to share, each with the other.

Some of the teenagers from the twenty-two-country Hugh O'Brian Youth Foundation Survey wanted to address their messages directly to adults, especially their parents:

> "Teenagers need to have a positive outlook. A lot of times, adults tell us how bleak the outlook is . . . to scare us into trying harder. Unfortunately, this puts too much pressure on kids, especially since we're already self-motivated and working hard. When they tell us depressing stuff, we get stressed out and depressed."
>
> *HOBY Participant, 15*

> "I want to know how to make parents understand teenagers in terms of change, growth, and originality."
>
> *HOBY Participant, 16*

> " . . . How to reach adults."
>
> *HOBY Participant, 15*

> "My parents should realize that I am the most responsible teenager I know, and many of my peers feel the same. How do I get my family to believe this about me?"
>
> *HOBY Participant, 16*

" . . . How to get adults, especially parents, to pay more attention to us."

HOBY Participant, 16

" . . . How to make parents take us seriously."

HOBY Participant, 16

Still other teenagers who contributed to the research of this book wanted to add one final thought about being the member of a group:

"When teenagers pick their groups they need to remember that, at first, all of the members of the group have a 'happy face' and are acting on their best behavior. Once teens participate, they will find out what the people in the group are really all about."

Paul, 19, Cultural

"Some of us teenagers are stuck 'between groups,' and this can be as tough as having no group at all. Mine are totally opposite of each other. So what I've learned is to make my own individual choices, because when it comes down to it, the group only 'reflects' me. The 'real me' comes from inside me."

Mayte, 19, Cultural and "Other" Group

"Group membership isn't about 'membership.' It's about being yourself and finding others who can accept that in you."

Karim, 17, Leadership

Two parents had messages—with different parental perspectives—that they wanted to share with their teens, and other parents:

"It's tougher to be a teenager—and be the parent of a teenager—than ever before. I made a conscious choice not to have my own children for these and other reasons. I feel blessed, however, that I have five wonderful step-daughters who have helped me redefine my ideas about life in the nineties and beyond. I have learned to experience parenthood, with all of its ups and downs, and wouldn't trade it for the world."

Judy, Step-Mother
Ari, 19, Social (and four other step-daughters)

"Familyhood is critical in the life of young people. Mothers and fathers need to be more willing to come home and find joy in parenting. When parents are eighty-five years old, rocking in their chairs, they will look back over their lives and wonder: "What was it all about?" And they will be the most proud of the ways they have influenced others' lives, not how much money they made, titles they earned, or external accomplishments. They will recall, with the greatest fondness, their roles as parents, and the affect they had on their children."

Ginger, Mother
Amy, 15, Religious (and seven other children)

Bibliography

Atanasoff, Stevan E. *How to Survive as a Teen: When No One Understands*. Scottdale, Pa.: Herald Press, 1989.

Bauman, Dr. Lawrence. *The Nine Most Troublesome Teenage Problems and How to Solve Them*. New York: Ballantine Books, 1986.

Branden, Nathaniel. *The Power of Self-Esteem*. Deerfield Beach, Fla.: Health Communications, Inc., 1992.

Borthwick, Paul. *But You Don't Understand*. Nashville: Oliver-Nelson, 1991.

Boyer, Ruth G. *The Happy Adolescent*. San Jose, Calif.: R&E Publishing, 1981.

Brondino, Jeanne. *Raising Each Other*: A Book for Parents and Teens. Claremont, Calif.: Borgo Press, 1989.

Campbell, David. *If You Don't Know Where You're Going, You'll Probably End Up Somewhere Else*. Allen, Tex.: Tabor Publishing, 1974.

Cohen, Daniel and Susan Cohen. *Teenage Stress: Understanding the Tensions You Feel at Home, at School and Among Your Friends*. New York: M. Evans & Co., Inc., 1983.

Coombs, H. Samm. *Teenage Survival Manual*. Lagunitas, Calif.: Discovery Books, Inc., 1989.

Crutsinger, Carla. *Teenage Connection: A Tool for Effective Teenage Communication*. Carrollton, Tex.: Brainworks, Inc., 1987.

Curran, Dolores. *Stress and the Healthy Family*. San Francisco: Harper San Francisco, 1987.

Dinkmeyer, Dr. Don and Dr. Gary D. McKay. *Raising a Responsible Child*. New York: A Fireside Book, 1973.

Domash, Leanne and Judith Sachs. *"Wanna Be My Friend?"* New York: Hearst Books, 1994.

Dumont, Larry. *Surviving Adolescence*. New York: Villard Books, 1991.

Elkind, David. *The Hurried Child*. Reading, Mass.: Addison-Wesley, 1988.

Elkind, David. *All Grown Up and No Place to Go*. Reading, Mass.: Addison-Wesley, 1984.

Eyre, Linda and Richard Eyre. *Teaching Your Children Values*. New York: Fireside, 1993.

Faber, Adele and Elaine Mazlish. *How to Talk So Kids Will Listen and Listen So Kids will Talk*. New York: Avon Books, 1980.

Felton Tracy, Louise. *Grounded for Life?!* Seattle: Parenting Press, Inc., 1994.

Fishel, Elizabeth. *I Swore I'd Never Do That!* Berkeley, Calif.: Conari Press, 1991.

Fleming, Don and Laurel J. Schmidt. *How to Stop the Battle with Your Teenager*. New York: Fireside, 1989.

Gabor, Don. *How to Start a Conversation and Make Friends*. New York: Fireside, 1983.

Garrod, Andrew, et al. *Adolescent Portraits: Cases in Identity, Relationships, and Challenges*. Needham Heights, Mass.: Allyn and Bacon, Inc., 1992.

Ginott, Haim G. *Between Parent and Teenager*. New York: Avon Books, 1971.

Ginott, Haim G. *Teacher and Child*. New York: Collier Books, 1993.

Gottlieb, Daniel and Edward Claflin. *Voices in the Family*. New York: Signet, 1991.

Hayes, E. Kent. *Why Good Parents Have Bad Kids*. New York: Doubleday, 1989.

Hauser, Stuart T., et al. *Adolescents and Their Families: Paths of Ego Development*. New York: Free Press, 1991.

Hearn, Janice W. *Making Friends, Keeping Friends*. Garden City, N.Y.: Doubleday-Galilee Original, 1979.

Jeffers, Susan. *Feel the Fear and Do It Anyway*. New York: Fawcett Columbine, 1987.

Keltner, Nancy. *If You Print This, Please Don't Use My Name: Questions from Teens and Their Parents about Things That Matter*. Davis, Calif.: Terra Nova, 1992.

Kirshenbaum, Mira and Charles Foster. *Parent-Teen Breakthrough*. New York: Plume, 1991.

Klein, Allen. *The Healing Power of Humor*. New York: Jeremy P. Tarcher/Perigee, 1989.

Kramer, Patricia. *Discovering Self-Confidence*. New York: Rosen Group, 1991.

Lang, Denise V. *But Everyone Else Looks So Sure of Themselves*. Crozet, Va.: Shoe Tree Press, 1991.

Leefeldt, Christine and Ernest Callenbach. *The Art of Friendship*. New York: Pantheon Books, 1979.

Lickona, Dr. Thomas. *Raising Good Children*. New York: Bantam Books, 1983.

Louv, Richard. *101 Things You Can Do for Our Children's Future*. New York: Anchor Book, 1994.

MacKenzie, Robert. *Setting Limits*. Rocklin, Calif.: Prima Publishing, 1993.

Madaras, Linda and Area Madaras. *My Feelings, My Self*. New York: Newmarket Press, 1993.

McGuire, J. Victor. *No Negatives: A Positive Guide to Successful Leadership*. Aurora, Colo.: Spice Press, 1989.

Nelson, Jane and Lynn Lott. *I'm on Your Side*. Rocklin, Calif.: Prima Publishing, 1991.

Nielson, Linda. *Adolescence: A Contemporary View*. Fort Worth, Tex.: Harcourt Brace College Publisher, 1991.

Phelan, Thomas W. *Surviving Your Adolescents*. Glen Ellyn, Ill.: Child Management, Inc., 1993.

Quindlen, Anna. *Raising Kids in a Changing World*. New York: Prentice Hall Press, 1991.

Ramsey, Patricia G. *Making Friends in School*. New York: Teachers College Press, 1991.

Rinzler, Jane. *Teens Speak Out: A Report from Today's Teen on Their Most Intimate Thoughts, Feelings and Hopes for the Future*. New York: Fine, Donald I., Inc., 1986.

Salzman, Marian and Teresa Reisgies. *One Hundred Fifty Ways Teens Can Make a Difference*. Princeton, N.J.: Peterson's Guides, 1991.

Seltzer, Vivian C. *Psychosocial Worlds of the Adolescent: Public & Private*. New York: Wiley, John and Sons, Inc., 1989.

Sheperd, Scott. *What Do You Think of You? A Teen's Guide to Finding Self-Esteem*. Minneapolis: CompCare, 1990.

Strasburger, Victor. *Getting Your Kids to Say "No" in the '90s When You Said "Yes" in the '60s*. New York: A Fireside Book, 1993.

Walsh, David. *Selling Out America's Children*. Minneapolis: Fairview Press, 1994.

Willeford, Stephen D. and Ruth H. Smith. *Teenagers and Peer Pressure*. Abilene, Tex.: Quality Publishers, 1984.

Wolf, Dr. Anthony E. *Get Out of My Life*. New York: The Noonday Press, 1991.

Youngs, Bettie B. and Brian S. Tracy. *Achievement, Happiness, Popularity and Success: A Self-Esteem Book for Young People*. Solana Beach, Calif.: Phoenix Educational Foundation, 1989.

Index

accept, 12, 18-19, 26, 34-35, 41, 47, 49, 53, 78, 81, 83, 85-86, 89, 92-93, 99, 108, 121, 123, 125-26, 130, 149, 158-59, 163, 173, 181, 191

accomplishment, 82, 98-100, 153

accountability, 39, 42, 178
    accountable, 76, 101

achievement, 108, 180, 195
    personal, 108

action, 26, 30, 38-40, 53, 56, 66, 75, 85, 88-90, 96-98, 104, 123, 136, 148, 155, 158, 174, 178, 186
    corrective, 97
    positive, 178
    punitive, 97
    take, 26, 97, 148, 186

activity, 29, 34, 48, 54, 56, 62, 67, 72, 79, 84, 87, 94, 96, 128, 133, 143
    ill-received, 96
    shared, 62, 67, 128

addiction, 78

adolescence, 3, 12, 17, 24, 27, 30, 33, 48, 64, 92, 103-4, 106-7, 109-10, 113-17, 119, 121, 127, 132, 145, 155, 157, 165, 168, 173-74, 177, 181, 184, 186, 188-89, 193, 195
    concept of, 116, 119

adolescent, 12, 63, 74, 91, 103, 109, 114, 118-19, 149, 154, 157, 168, 174, 179-81, 183-85,

188, 193-95
    revolution, 118

adulthood, 2-4, 12, 26, 28, 56, 68, 103, 107, 110, 116, 118, 167-68, 173, 177, 188
    answers about, 167, 177

affirmation, 85-86
    process of, 86

aggression, 135
    parental, 135

aggressive, 185, 189
    aggressiveness, 102
    parenthood, 185, 189

anger, 39, 94-95, 104, 106, 159-60, 165
    and sadness, 106

approval-seekers, 22

argument, 93

assert, 20, 25, 27, 30, 54, 73, 88, 90, 94-95, 103-4, 110, 140
    teens . . . themselves, 103

assertive, 79, 95, 140-44, 150, 154-55
    behavior, 140-41, 144, 154-55
    communication, 142, 155
    communicators, 144
    listening, 150
    parents, 141

assertiveness, 23, 104, 140-42, 144-45, 155
    skillful, 144
    verbal, 142

attitude, 56, 66, 78, 138

authoritative parents, 94, 160, 166
combative, 93
overcritical, 93
over-controlling, 94
responsible, 95
parental duties, 115
parenthood, 117, 185, 189, 192
parenting, 93-95, 109, 117-19, 123, 140, 158, 165, 173, 177, 192, 194
consciousness, 117
entire parenting experience, 158
form of, 94
good, 173
responsible, 95
part-time, 118
positive, 173, 177
styles, 93, 95, 109, 123, 158, 165
patience, 11, 53, 172-173, 178, 182
peer, 34-35, 37, 42, 44-45, 47, 49, 51, 53-57, 59-61, 92, 101, 110, 163, 166, 173, 180-82, 188, 195
approval, 51, 56, 60
bonding, 181, 188
counsel, 37
groups, 55-56, 163, 166, 173
impact, 34, 44-45, 47, 49, 51, 53, 55, 57, 59, 61
influence, 56, 61
negative . . . pressure, 53-55, 60
pressure, 51, 53-55, 60, 195
relationship-building, 51
shock, 34-35, 42
personal development, 4, 7, 12, 47, 53-54, 60, 117
personality, 35, 69, 98
perspective, 35, 75-76, 92, 100, 104, 128, 163, 187
other people's, 101

place and space, 70
popular, 22, 25, 47-48, 50, 67, 83, 173, 179-80, 182, 188
popularity, 17, 48, 179-83, 188-89, 195
hopes for, 182
pressure of, 183
ratings, 180
test, 181
positive, 6, 10, 13, 15, 17-18, 26, 31, 40, 45, 49, 55, 67-68, 72, 74-76, 78-79, 83, 85-86, 88-90, 98, 101-2, 104, 107-11, 113-14, 118, 123, 133-34, 138-41, 143-44, 153-56, 158, 164-66, 168, 170-71, 173-74, 176-78, 181, 186-87, 190, 195
affirmations, 86
attitude, 138
attitudes and actions, 173
decisions, 141
definitions of themselves, 181
difference, 109, 111, 186
direction, 165
example, 170
outlook, 190
parenting, 173, 177
reinforcement, 102, 107, 110
results, 40, 74, 98, 101, 143, 156
thinking, 85, 88
thoughts, 76, 78, 85, 89
power, 4, 14-17, 19-21, 23, 25, 27, 40, 47, 56, 59-61, 67, 75, 77, 85, 91-93, 95, 97, 99, 101-5, 107-11, 138, 140, 144, 158, 167, 193-94
friendship and, 102
higher, 91
of their dreams, 108
perception of, 102
positions of, 167
searching for, , 92
struggle for, 91, 102, 109, 110
teenagers pursue, 102